Survival Guide for Coaching Youth Football

Jim Dougherty
Brandon Castel

Human Kinetics

Library of Congress Cataloging-in-Publication Data

Dougherty, Jim.
  Survival guide for coaching youth football / Jim Dougherty and Brandon Castel.
    p. cm.
  ISBN-13: 978-0-7360-9113-8 (soft cover)
  ISBN-10: 0-7360-9113-0 (soft cover)
  1. Youth league football--Coaching. I. Castel, Brandon. II. Title.
  GV959.6.D68 1992
  796.33--dc22

                         2010012423

ISBN-10: 0-7360-9113-0 (print)
ISBN-13: 978-0-7360-9113-8 (print)

Acquisitions Editor: Justin Klug; **Developmental Editor:** Heather Healy; **Assistant Editor:** Michael Bishop; **Copyeditor:** Patricia MacDonald; **Permission Manager:** Martha Gullo; **Graphic Designer:** Nancy Rasmus; **Graphic Artist:** Julie L. Denzer; **Cover Designer:** Keith Blomberg; **Photographer (interior):** Neil Bernstein; **Visual Production Assistant:** Joyce Brumfield; **Photo Production Manager:** Jason Allen; **Art Manager:** Kelly Hendren; **Associate Art Manager:** Alan L. Wilborn; **Printer:** Sheridan Books

We thank the University of Illinois in Urbana, Illinois, for assistance in providing the location for the photo shoot for this book.

We thank Jamal Maatuka, Khalfani Maatuka, Jabali Maatuka, Jeremy Rumsey, Luke Luffman, Jake Luffman, Seth Richmond, and Jaden Roberts for their assistance with the photo shoot.

Printed in the United States of America   10 9 8 7 6 5 4 3 2 1

The paper in this book is certified under a sustainable forestry program.

Human Kinetics
Web site: www.HumanKinetics.com

United States: Human Kinetics
P.O. Box 5076
Champaign, IL 61825-5076
800-747-4457
e-mail: humank@hkusa.com

Canada: Human Kinetics
475 Devonshire Road Unit 100
Windsor, ON N8Y 2L5
800-465-7301 (in Canada only)
e-mail: info@hkcanada.com

Europe: Human Kinetics
107 Bradford Road
Stanningley
Leeds LS28 6AT, United Kingdom
+44 (0) 113 255 5665
e-mail: hk@hkeurope.com

Australia: Human Kinetics
57A Price Avenue
Lower Mitcham, South Australia 5062
08 8372 0999
e-mail: info@hkaustralia.com

New Zealand: Human Kinetics
P.O. Box 80
Torrens Park, South Australia 5062
0800 222 062
e-mail: info@hknewzealand.com

E5077

Survival Guide for Coaching Youth Football

 # Contents

Drill Finder

Drill title	Beginner	Intermediate	Advanced	Quarterbacks	Centers	Running backs	Receivers	Offensive line	Defensive line	Linebackers	Defensive backs	Page no.
	Skill level			Offense					Defense			
Taking the snap	✔			✔	✔							59
Partner passing		✔		✔								60
Quarterback footwork			✔	✔								62
Stance and release	✔					✔	✔					64
Cutting		✔				✔	✔					66
Bad ball	✔						✔					68
One-hand catch		✔					✔					69
Power step	✔							✔				70
Angle step	✔							✔				71
Pull step		✔						✔				72
Slalom course	✔								✔	✔	✔	91
Come to balance	✔								✔	✔	✔	92
Angle tackle		✔							✔	✔	✔	93
Oklahoma			✔						✔	✔	✔	94
Explosive step	✔								✔			95
Tennis ball drop		✔							✔			96
Man in the mirror		✔								✔		97
The tip			✔							✔	✔	98
The W			✔							✔	✔	99
Zigzag		✔									✔	100

# Preface

For some, football is about winning and losing. Legendary coach Vince Lombardi once asked, "If winning isn't everything, why do they keep score?" He coached the Green Bay Packers to five world championships. You, in all likelihood, will not.

You have decided, however, that it's time to get out of the house and tackle the world of coaching. What better place to start than with the bright smiling faces of America's youth. You volunteered to coach a local youth football team, only now you're in a room full of 8- and 9-year-olds, and those faces aren't looking so bright all of a sudden. For many first-time coaches, this can be a tense situation—a fight or flight moment as they weigh their options: *Can I really do this? What if I'm not ready? What if they're not ready? Where is the nearest exit? Can I really outrun a group of 9-year-olds at my age?*

These are all natural reactions for someone facing the daunting task of molding a boisterous group of youngsters for the first time, but it doesn't have to be that way. Coaching youth football can be one of the most exciting and rewarding experiences of your life if you are ready. Like most things in life, preparation is the key to success. This book is designed to help you, the rookie coach, prepare for what it takes to help kids aged 6 to 10 play the game of football.

Maybe you were the star of your high school football team, but just being an elite athlete is not enough. Not all great football players make great football coaches. Just because you know how to play the game at a high level doesn't mean you will be able to teach these kids how to do the same. Whether you were the quarterback of your team in college or are a saxophone player who has always admired the sport from a distance, this book will teach you how to teach your players the fundamentals of football in a way that is both fun and enlightening.

It might not seem like it when they are busy chattering away while throwing dirt at each other, but kids love to play and to learn—whether they admit it or not. Most of them will know the basics of throwing and catching—and maybe they know that if they get in the end zone it's a touchdown—but beyond that it is up to you to mold and shape their minds around the complex sport of football. You will teach them not only the basics of the game, but also how to be a part of a team, something many of them have not experienced outside of the classroom before.

It might sound impossible to turn a group of unruly kids into a cohesive unit with a united goal, but you are the envy of the coaching world. Coaches at the higher levels inherit quarterbacks who already have a kink in their throwing motions or defensive backs who already have a habit of turning their backs to the ball, and these coaches have to reteach their players the right way of doing things. You, on the other hand, are one of the privileged few. By getting these kids at such a young age, you won't have to deal with bad habits they picked up somewhere else. So instead of correcting bad stances and poor form, you get to start from scratch by teaching them the fundamentals of playing football. Although that is a dream for most coaches, it can also be a bit intimidating. Because bad habits will be harder to break down the road, it's your job to make sure these kids start off on the right foot, so to speak.

And that's where this book comes in. It would hardly be fair to put the weight of these kids' football futures on your shoulders without giving you the tools to shape them with. There are plenty of books out there aimed at teaching athletes how to take their game to the next level. This is not one of them. Too often athletes reach the middle school and high school levels without the proper fundamental training they need. Their coaches can read books on how to make these players better, but they can't go back in time and teach them the fundamentals they needed to learn at an early age.

This book will help you make sure the kids you coach are getting those fundamentals so they can fulfill their greatest potential as football players. In the following chapters you will find everything a first-time coach needs to keep from losing his head. Whether it's the guide to equipment and safety in chapter 1, the detailed practice plan in chapter 2, or the skill and team development plans given throughout the rest of the chapters, this book will be your survival guide on the path to success.

Key to Diagrams

Coach

→ Run

⊢ Block

Presnap motion

Pass

Pitch

Handoff or fake handoff

Football

Blocking bag

Cone

Offense

Any offensive player

Left tackle

Left guard

Center

Right guard

Right tackle

Tight end

Quarterback

Running back

Fullback

Wide receiver

Receiver

Defense

 Any defensive player

 Defensive end

 Nose tackle

 Defensive tackle

 Linebacker

 Cornerback

 Strong safety

 Free safety

Special teams

 Long snapper

 Gunner

 Punt coverage player

 Punter

 Holder

 Kicker

Help! Where Do I Start?

As a rookie coach, much of your focus leading up to the first practice will be on what you are going to do and say when the time finally comes. There are a few basics, however, that a coach must have organized before he blows his first whistle. The basics can cover anything from making sure your players have the proper equipment to making sure they have enough water. There's nothing worse than getting everyone to the field and finding out it's already taken, so knowing where and when to practice is just as important as knowing how to practice. These things seem basic, but they are often overlooked. This chapter helps you stay focused on what needs to be done in the preseason.

Essential Equipment

Football is a contact sport. It is viewed by some as a violent and barbaric sport that appeals only to the most gruesome parts of human nature. Yet, today's game is a much safer and more civilized version of what it was just a century ago. Back then, all a player needed was a leather helmet, which probably explains why nearly 20 college kids died from playing football in 1905. Big hits and broken bones will always be a part of the sport, but today, the game is about safety. And that means having the right protection for your players. As a coach, you will need access to the following equipment:

- **First aid kit.** This is a must-have for any coach, at any level, in any sport. Bring it to all practices and games, and keep it near the action at all times. You can likely pick up a good kit with all the essentials at a local sporting goods store, or you can piece one together yourself. Kids are going to get cuts and scrapes, and the very sight of blood is enough to send practice into an uproar, so every first aid kit should start with Band-Aids. It should also include a pair of latex gloves, 4-inch (10 cm) sterile gauze bandages (this will come in handy for bloody noses), and a tube of antiseptic ointment for cleaning cuts. Most first aid kits should also include disinfectant wipes and adhesive tape for taping bandages or fingers.

- **Whistle.** Get one. It doesn't matter how funny you think you are or how riveting the speech you prepared the night before may be, kids are going to lose interest. It's just what they do. As much as they may love football, they also love kicking dirt, throwing grass, and watching the geese that just wandered onto the field. Something as simple as an anthill can send 20 kids into a frenzy of screams and laughter, so it's important to have a way to get their attention off the bugs and back on you.

- **Footballs.** This seems like a no-brainer, but you won't be laughing if you have to practice without them. If your league or field provides footballs, then you're good to go. If not, you will need to rent, buy, or borrow them; just make sure they are the right size for your league. Companies such as Wilson, Rawlings, Franklin, and Spalding produce different size footballs for different ages. If you are coaching in a league with kids younger than 9 years old (also known as Pee Wee), you will probably be using K2 footballs, which you can find at any sporting goods store. If you're coaching in a league for 9- to 12-year-olds (also known as Pop Warner), you will likely be using TDJ (junior) footballs, which are a little larger than K2 balls. Step up to a league for 12- to 14-year-olds and you're looking at TDY (youth) footballs, and anything older than that will probably use standard collegiate footballs.

  The number of footballs you will need depends on the size of your roster. Ideally, you should have a minimum of one football for every two players so they can warm up by tossing the football with a partner. You can always go with more, but try to avoid going with fewer; the more footballs you have, the less standing around you will have in practice (and thus less time for kids to find other things to occupy their attention).

  You'll want a mesh bag or a large gym bag to carry the balls in, and it's a good idea to keep them in your car so you never have to worry about arriving at practice without them. You won't need as many on game days, but you should still bring a few balls to warm up with. Make sure at least one of them is a good ball because some leagues require you to use your own football when your team has the ball.

- **Cones.** It's a good idea to come equipped with cones. Most kids have no concept of distance or football terminology. If you tell three different kids to go 10 yards deep for a pass, one kid is going to run 2 feet (.6 m) and turn around, another will run to the opposite end of the field, and the last one will just stand there looking at you. Cones are a good way of marking off accurate distances that will allow kids to visualize the difference between 5, 20, and 50 yards.

- **Pads and helmets.** If you are in a league that does not allow pads and helmets, then you won't need to worry about this. Most leagues, however, are going to require pads and helmets, which makes equipment day one of the most important things you do in the preseason. Some leagues will supply all of the equipment, which means they should send someone out to do all the sizing and fitting for your team. If you have to do this on your own, you need to learn how to size helmets and equipment. If parents are providing the equipment for their child, they may have a tendency to buy big so their kid can grow into it as he gets older. If that is the case, you may need an insert for the helmet because it needs to fit snugly to be safe.

  We recommend going to a local sporting goods dealer and inviting someone who knows what he is doing to come out and measure the kids for their equipment (you can even try calling someone at Riddell, Wilson, or whoever supplies your equipment, and the company may be happy to send someone out). You might have to pay the person, but a half-hour of his time will save a lot of headaches. Keep in mind that you may not be allowed to have the players practice in full pads the first day. Even if you are allowed, it's not a good idea to do so.

- **Mouth guards.** If your kids are going to be doing any tackling, they will need mouth guards. These will be especially important as the kids advance to higher levels of football, but they are also vital in the beginning stages. The mouth guards are going to feel a little uncomfortable at first, so this will be a good chance for kids to get used to wearing them. In most cases the parents can use the old-fashioned approach of dipping the mouth guard in boiling water for five seconds, dropping it in cold water for a second, and then having the kid bite down and suck the air out of it.

The league you are in may provide mouth guards, but more likely than not it will be on you and the parents to make sure every kid has one. Most brands are cheap and can be purchased at any sporting goods store or even Walmart, so it might not be a bad idea to just go ahead and grab enough for your team (or at least some extras) next time you're at the store. In some special cases, the kid may need to see an orthodontist to get a two-part mouthpiece, but that would be at the discretion of the parents.

- **Water.** Most leagues will play in the late summer or early fall, and that means your players will need water, and lots of it. Keeping these kids hydrated should be one of your top priorities, right after keeping them safe. Even if there are water fountains available at the field, it is smart to have the kids bring their own water bottles from home. This is where the parents come in. Make it clear to them how important it is that their kids bring enough water to practice. If the field doesn't have water fountains, then it's a good idea for you to bring a cooler full of water as a backup, even if that means removing a seat from your car so that everything will fit.

- **Blocking bags.** Not all leagues will have practice fields with blocking bags readily available, but if you can find one that does, it will be a tremendous benefit to your practice time. Blocking bags or sleds help coaches teach the fundamentals of blocking and tackling while simulating contact without the risk of injury.

Know the League Regulations

Now that you've got your car packed to the roof with cones, footballs, a water cooler, and the rest of the gear, you need to get familiar with a few other league regulations. First, you must know how much time you will have to practice. If you are working for a school, or if your team is part of a league, then practice time and a field are usually provided. Either way, being prepared and staying organized are the two most important things a coach can do to get ready for practice. Stuff is going to happen that you can't control. How you respond will depend on how you prepared. To get ready for your practice sessions, you will need to know the following:

- **Practice time.** How many practices a week? How many minutes per practice? Some youth leagues limit practice days, so this may not be up to you. Ideally, you would like to practice two days in pads and one day out of pads during the week, but you may have to settle for less. With this age group, practices should last no longer than 90 minutes, so it's important to have a practice plan in mind. (Don't worry; we will help you organize your practices in the next chapter.) If the league allows you to practice more than three times during the week, keep in mind these are young kids, and they have other things to do with their time besides football practice.

- **Field usage.** If you're fortunate enough to have an official field on which to practice, hopefully you won't have to share it. If you are splitting the field with another team, it's not the end of the world. Try to split it down the middle at the 50-yard line so that each team has half of a regulation field to work with. Most of the drills in this book can be accomplished within the framework of a shorter field. Many times you won't be lucky enough to have a full-size regulation field for practice. Football season heats up in late July and early August, and youth teams often take a backseat to the older groups that need more preparation. If possible, get your team on a field with lines already marked for the yardage, end zones, and hash marks (see figure 1.1). This will help kids become more comfortable with the layout of the field that they will see on game days, and it will give you the chance to teach them the different parts of the field.

- **Weight limits.** For the longest time, most Pee Wee and Pop Warner football leagues had weight restrictions to go along with their age limitations as a way to help prevent injuries. Today, more and more leagues are allowing bigger kids to play with other kids the same age because of how much damage it can do to their self-esteem. Check with your league to find out if there are any such weight restrictions.

- **Coach participation.** Some leagues will allow coaches to be on the field and even in the huddle with their teams. Usually this is reserved for the Pee Wee level (6 to 9 years old), but even some Pop Warner leagues allow a coach to be involved in calling the plays on the field. This is just another detail you should find out from the league before you start practicing.

Protect Yourself and Your Players

Your biggest administrative duty is dealing with the medical side of sports. Football is a contact sport. Injuries are going to happen, so it is important that you protect not only your players but yourself as well. Many leagues will require your players to provide proof of insurance before their first game, as well as a waiver form signed by their parents. If your league does not require these documents, you should still consider making them a prerequisite for the players on your team.

It is also a good idea to have medical cards like the one shown in figure 1.2 on file for each kid, along with a copy of his annual physical. These will prove vital in the case of a medical emergency. The medical cards should include emergency phone numbers, doctor's information, and any existing medical conditions, particularly those that might require medication to be administered during practice. These forms should be kept with you at all times whenever the team is meeting (it might be easiest to keep them with your first aid kit). Having them in your car or at home in a file does no good for you or the player should a medical situation arise.

It is also important to keep your cell phone nearby for a quick 911 call in case of emergency. Football is a sport designed to have high-speed collisions, so it's particularly important that a coach have some kind of first aid training. Some leagues and parks will require coaches to be certified in first aid. Even if yours does not, a CPR class through the American Heart Association or the American Red Cross is highly recommended. Emergency response teams will get there as quickly as possible, but every second counts in a medical crisis. As the adult on the scene, you are the first line of defense, and your ability to respond until the paramedics arrive could make the difference.

Most injuries you encounter as a coach will be minor bumps and bruises. Bloody noses and sprained ankles are about the worst of it, more often than not. Occasionally, however, you will be faced with a serious injury. Broken bones, separations, and dislocations are a part of football, so it is important to be ready for them. Notifying the parents and calling 911 should be your first plan of attack. In the event of a head or neck injury, it is imperative not to move the player until paramedics arrive. Do not even try to remove his helmet unless the player is up and walking around or he is not breathing.

Even with the extra padding inside football helmets today, concussions are a very real part of the game. Even at this level, where hits rarely happen at the type of speed you would expect to result in a concussion,

Figure 1.2   Sample Medical Card

Player's Information

Player's name: _____

Allergies, medications, and other important medical information: ____

_____

_____

Medical Authorization

Part I (to grant consent)

In the event that reasonable attempts to contact me or the alternative contact have been unsuccessful, I hereby give my consent (1) for the administration of any treatment deemed necessary by our physician or dentist, or in the event that the designated preferred practitioner is not available, by another licensed physician or dentist, and (2) for the transfer of the child to our preferred hospital or one that is reasonably accessible. This authorization does not cover major surgery unless the medical opinions of two physicians or dentists, concurring in the necessity for such surgery, are obtained before surgery is performed.

Preferred doctor's name: _____

Phone: _____

Preferred hospital: _____

Preferred dentist's name: _____

Phone: _____

Signature of parent or guardian: _____

Date:_____ Print name: _____

Part II (refusal to consent to treatment)
Do not complete part II if you completed part I.

I DO NOT give my consent for emergency medical treatment of the child in the event of illness or injury requiring treatment. I wish the coaching staff to take no action or to: _____

_____

Signature of parent or guardian: _____

Date: _____ Print name: _____

From J. Dougherty and B. Castel, 2010, *Survival Guide for Coaching Youth Football* (Champaign, IL: Human Kinetics).

a helmet-to-helmet collision can be a scary moment for any coach. Concussions are very serious because they change the way the brain functions, and you should not wait until after practice to address these injuries. Even if a player never loses consciousness, he could still be concussed. Table 1.1 provides the symptoms an athlete may experience or those you may notice in a player. If a child exhibits any of these signs after a collision, you should immediately notify the parents and call 911.

In addition to the previously mentioned injuries, consider familiarizing yourself with medical conditions such as a diabetes, asthma, and epilepsy. For example, if a player you know to be diabetic becomes shaky, pale, clammy, dizzy, or disoriented, it is important to pull him out of practice. Call 911 immediately, and alert the player's parents. Along those same lines, one of the scariest things that can happen to a coach is for one of his players to have an epileptic seizure during practice. It not only is frightening for the other players but also causes coaches to feel helpless. In this situation, it is best to move the other players and objects away from the child while calling 911 and the parents. (Notice a theme developing here?)

Table 1.1   Concussion Symptoms

Signs observed by coaching staff	Symptoms reported by athlete
Appears dazed or stunned	Headache or "pressure" in head
Is confused about assignment or position	Nausea or vomiting
Forgets sports plays	Balance problems or dizziness
Is unsure of game, score, or opponent	Double or blurry vision
Moves clumsily	Sensitivity to light
Answers questions slowly	Sensitivity to noise
Loses consciousness (even briefly)	Feeling sluggish, hazy, foggy, or groggy
Shows behavior or personality changes	Concentration or memory problems
Can't recall events prior to hit or fall	Confusion
Can't recall events after hit or fall	Does not "feel right"

Adapted from M.R. Lovell, et al., *The American Journal of Sports Medicine* 32(1), pp. 47-54, copyright © 2004 by American Orthopaedic Society for Sports Medicine. Reprinted with permission of Sage Publications.

Involve the Parents

Parents can be either a coach's best allies or his worst enemies. For the most part, it's up to you. It is best to get parents on your side right from the start because if you end up on their bad side, you had better dig yourself a foxhole and hunker down for the fight of your life. Most parents are overprotective—and rightly so—of their children, especially at a young age, so it's your job to put them at ease. This can best be done by being up front about everything right from the start. A preseason parents-only meeting is the best way to prevent potential issues that could creep up later in the season. It gives the parents a chance to meet the person who will be coaching their children; and it gives you, the coach, a chance to set expectations for both the players and the parents heading into the season.

This is the best opportunity to provide the parents with your contact information: home phone, work phone, cell phone, and e-mail. Make sure they know which one is the best way to get in touch with you for different reasons (e.g., cell phone for emergencies, e-mail for general questions). It is also a chance for you to get all of their relevant information at the same time to keep on file. The sample information card in figure 1.3 can help you gather what you need. (Make sure to get their e-mail addresses if you plan to send out weekly updates of practice schedules and game times.) After a brief introduction of yourself and your background, it is time to lay the foundation for what you expect this season and what the parents can expect from you. The more you cover here, the more at ease the parents will be. It's important to keep in mind that for many of these parents, this is their first experience with contact football. If you don't do well speaking in front of big groups (of adults), practice in front of a mirror. Be prepared, and know what you want to say.

Let the parents know you will need their help in running the team. If possible, establish a practice start time and practice end time. Make it clear to the parents that start time does not mean arrival time. For example, if you plan to practice at 6:00 p.m., you should tell the parents to arrive by 5:45 p.m. If you simply tell them practice starts at six, you can be sure some parents will pull into the parking lot at 6:05. It is also important to point out the need for punctual pickups. You don't want parents coming too early and honking the horn in the parking lot with five minutes left in practice. You also don't want them coming too late. Be sure to point out that if they are not there to pick up their kids when practice ends, you

Figure 1.3   Sample Information Card

Player's Information

Player's name: _____

Date of birth: _____

People to call when player is ill or in case of emergency:

Main contact (parent or guardian): _____

Home phone: _____   Work phone: _____

Cell phone: _____

E-mail address: _____

Address: _____

Preferred method of contact (circle one): e-mail / home phone / cell phone

Alternative contact: _____

Relationship to player: _____

Home phone: _____   Work phone: _____

Cell phone: _____

E-mail address: _____

Address: _____

Preferred method of contact (circle one): e-mail / home phone / cell phone

From J. Dougherty and B. Castel, 2010, *Survival Guide for Coaching Youth Football* (Champaign, IL: Human Kinetics).

or one of your coaches (assuming you are fortunate enough to have assistants) will have to stay and wait with their child. Some parents are quick to forget you are not a full-time coach. They assume you spend 12 hours a day at the field, so it's good to let them know you also have other things going on and cannot wait around 20 minutes after practice for parents who show up late.

Strive to maintain a regular practice schedule. If the parents are being courteous enough to drop off and pick up their kids on time, you should return the favor by sticking to a simple practice routine—such as 6:00 p.m. on Tuesdays and Thursdays—so that the parents can plan their schedules in advance. (It is still a good idea to e-mail a friendly reminder to the parents each week with the team's schedule for the upcoming week.) This will alleviate a lot of stress on you and on the parents who have rearranged their schedules to make sure their kids get to football practice.

It is also smart to set up a contingency plan in case of rain if you want to avoid getting 20 phone calls over a light afternoon drizzle. Make sure the parents know ahead of time that if it rains heavily on Tuesday, practice will either be canceled altogether or rescheduled for Wednesday. The choice is up to you, but be consistent. Under no circumstances should you ever practice in a thunderstorm where lightning has been spotted. Even games will be delayed or canceled in those situations. Practicing in light rain is acceptable, but keep in mind the age group you are working with; this is not big-time high school football, and you do not have a crucial game coming up this week, unless of course you are one of the O'Shea brothers. (If you haven't seen the movie *Little Giants*, be sure to put that on the to-do list before embarking on the journey of coaching youth football.)

Many problems arise because coaches do not set clear expectations for the players and parents before the season. Certain to be among the key issues are playing time, team goals, and parental involvement. It's important to let parents know your goal is to keep playing time as equal as possible. In all likelihood, the next Joe Montana is not on your team; but if you ask the parents, you might think there are 10 to 15 Joe Montanas all waiting for their chance to shine. Positions may not seem like a big deal, but they are significant to the players and parents. It's a good idea to assign positions early—that way kids can tell their parents and friends what position they are playing—but be sure to let the parents know you will be rotating kids through multiple positions.

Another good way to head off potential problems with parents is by letting them know what is expected of them on game days. You will undoubtedly have parents who are planning to relive the glory days of high school through this team, but you need to keep that competitive spirit from becoming a cutthroat mentality. Remind the parents this team is about developing fundamental skills, not necessarily about wins and losses. No kid is out there trying to make mistakes. They are all trying to do the best they can, so yelling at a kid—whether it is that parent's kid or another—is not going to help and will not be tolerated. Find a way to get the super-spirited parents involved in other ways. Put one or two of them in charge of organizing snacks and specialty drinks such as juice or

Gatorade for games. Find a parent who's really into taking pictures (and hopefully has some talent) and make her the official team photographer. Give someone else the role of party planning for a postseason gathering to celebrate a great season of sportsmanship and fun.

It might even be a good idea to appoint one or two parents as assistant coaches, as long as they understand and respect your authority as the head coach. In any event, make sure the parents know officials are there to officiate (no need to yell at them), coaches are there to coach (no need to second-guess them), and players are there to play (no need to put them down). If parents are not in one of these three categories, their job is to sit back and support the team from the stands in a positive manner.

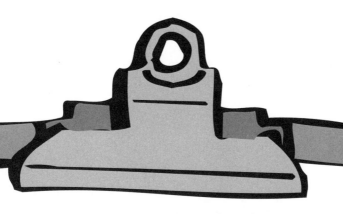

The Coach's Clipboard

✔ Preparation is the best disguise for inexperience.

✔ Football is a contact sport, so players should have the proper equipment at all times, whether it is a game or practice.

✔ First aid kits should include Band-Aids, latex gloves, sterile gauze bandages, and disinfectant wipes.

✔ Don't forget the practice essentials, such as footballs, cones, and even a whistle.

✔ Know the practice field and when it will be available for you and your team.

✔ Keep your players' completed medical cards and a cell phone with you at every practice and game.

✔ Be punctual and precise with parents so they know where they need to be with their kids and when they need to be there.

✔ Getting parents actively involved is a good way to head off potential problems with the overzealous ones.

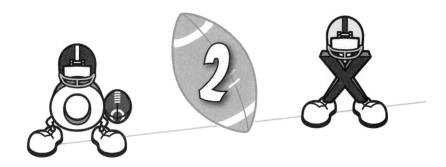

Organizing Your Team Practices

If you're reading this chapter, it means you've made it through the pre-season parents meeting in one piece. Kudos on a job well done, but now it's time to focus on their pride and joy. Even if you are blessed with a team full of future All-Americans, no group is ready to take to the field on day one. Coaching your team to a championship is about more than just calling the right plays on game day. It's about doing things in a fun manner that teaches your players the fundamentals of football, and it's also about practice. And before you can have a good practice, you need to have a good practice plan.

It might sound easy to line up 11 kids in an offensive formation and teach them to run a play, but what happens when three of your offensive linemen are playing leapfrog, your running back doesn't remember the play, and one of your wide receivers has wandered off onto the baseball diamond? Kids naturally have a short attention span. They are interested in doing just about anything they aren't allowed to do, but it's your job to get them focused on football.

As fun as the game might be, just learning how to play is not enough to keep a group of 5- to 10-year-olds occupied for 60 to 90 minutes. As a coach, you not only play the role of teacher during practice but also assume the role of entertainer. Although dressing up as SpongeBob SquarePants may seem like a good way to make sure all eyes are on you, not much football is being played under the sea these days, so a different plan of action is needed. The best strategy is to keep things moving along. Spending too much time on one drill or one concept can be counterproductive, and it's the quickest way to lose the kids' interest and open the door for mischief. Here are some additional strategies to keep the attention focused in your direction:

- **Employ active learning.** Remember that high school biology teacher who used to drone on in excruciating detail about chloroplasts and the process of photosynthesis? Don't be that guy. No matter how late you stay up writing the perfect speech for the next day, it's going to be wasted on these kids if it lasts longer than five minutes. The most effective way for children to process information is through active learning. It might sound like a good idea to cover everything in detail before you get started, but most of it is going to get lost. Remember that kids learn best when they are actively participating in what's being taught. If you want to demonstrate the right way to do something, find a kid who knows what he's doing and have him be the one to show the other kids. Ultimately, the goal should be to get as many kids participating in the drill as possible.

- **Use attention grabbers.** No matter how much fun they are having or how well you are keeping them involved in what's going on, kids are going to lose focus at one point or another during practice. Their minds are simply built to wander, so it's important to have some tricks up your sleeve when that happens. Using a magic word of the day, a chant, or a series of whistles are all good ways of letting the kids know it's time to be looking at the coach. Having them touch their noses or assume an athletic stance is a good way for the kids to show you who is listening and who needs to follow suit. The important thing is to make these attention grabbers fun and easy to understand.

- **Make the end of practice fun.** Another great way to grab their focus at the end of practice—when most kids will be worn out and all but done with football—is to have them play ultimate football, or speed football. This is a game that calls for a lot of running, so it's a great conditioner, but it also allows every kid the chance to pass, catch, and run. The objective of the game is to score touchdowns by passing the ball to a player in the end zone, but no one can run while holding the football (some variations allow the player to take three steps after catching the ball).

Surviving the First Practices

Preparing for your first game as a football coach can be both exciting and terrifying at the same time. After all, you probably wouldn't have signed up to coach this team if you didn't love the game of football, love working with young kids, or hopefully both. At the same time, that doesn't mean there won't be nerves that come with your first practices as a coach. Being organized is a big way to eliminate some of the anxiety that comes with being a rookie coach. It's important to keep things simple, especially in the first few practices. You're not going to build a championship contender overnight, so don't force it. Cramming their little brains with too much football is only going to cause a system overload, and all you're going to get are blank stares, or the equivalent of the blue screen of death. Instead, start with the basics. Use this time to lay the groundwork for the rest of your season.

Getting to Know Your Players

One of the first things you should do as a coach once practice begins is get to know the players you will be coaching while letting them get to know you. Remember that wide receiver who wandered off to the baseball diamond? It's going to be a lot easier to get him back with the rest of the team if you can call out his name instead of yelling, *Hey, kid!* in his general direction.

It's a good idea to introduce yourself and any assistant coaches you might be fortunate enough to have with you. Here's where having a personality will come in handy. You don't want to come across as the class clown, but having a sense of humor is a good way to win over some of the kids who might be a little hesitant to get involved. As a coach, it's important to have balance. You are a teacher first and a friend second, so set the tone early that the coach is in charge, but it's also important for the kids to feel as if they have an open line of communication with you and your staff. Ask lots of questions, and encourage the kids to do the same. Speak loudly and directly at the kids while making eye contact, and remember your audience. These are young kids, so use age-appropriate language and don't say anything you wouldn't want them to repeat at the family dinner table, because they most certainly will.

If you have a team of 20 or so kids, you probably can't learn all their names on day one—although you can certainly try—but it's important to get to know each kid's name over the course of the first few practices. One good idea—something you even see with NFL and college teams in training camp—is to write each kid's name on a piece of masking tape to put on the front of their helmets. This will help you visualize what each kid looks like in his gear, and it will help you yell out names instead of just numbers.

Playing an icebreaker game is a good way for you to learn their names and for the kids to learn each other's names, which will only help boost camaraderie among the team. One quick and easy icebreaker involves having the kids sit in one big circle. Go around the circle having each kid give his name along with a favorite food, animal, color, movie, and so on. The list of possibilities here is endless, so you should be able to come up with something new every day until you have mastered their names. Along with learning their names, you will get the chance to get a brief glimpse into each of their personalities, something that can prove vital for a coach when deciding how to instruct or correct a member of the team. Some kids will be reserved and apprehensive during the icebreaker, while others will be loud and obnoxious. Here is where you put on your psychologist hat as you analyze which kids need a pat on the back and which ones need a kick in the pants (figuratively not physically).

During the first few practices, you should also begin to get a sense of the differences in athletic ability among your players. If you are like most youth football coaches, the range of skill level on your roster when you first hit the practice field will be dramatic. Some kids will look as if they've been playing football for years, while others might have trouble just gripping the ball. This should give you an indication of which kids are ready to jump in and play right away, but don't confuse experience with talent. Just because a kid doesn't know how to throw a spiral yet doesn't necessarily mean he won't be an all-star quarterback once he learns.

No matter what the talent level of each child, let him know that hustle and effort are all that's really expected of him. It's your job to develop whatever talent he might have. It's all too common for coaches to be drawn to their most naturally gifted athletes, but don't make the mistake of ignoring the kid who makes up for his lack of athletic ability by working hard and playing smart. In fact, when you're dealing with kids this age that haven't even hit puberty yet, don't make the mistake of overlooking any of them; you never really know how kids are going to develop, and it's not your job to play Nostradamus. Teach every kid the fundamentals he might need to advance in the sport, and don't be selective with your knowledge or your time.

Sizing Up Your Team

Now that you've got a better idea of who these kids are, you've got to start making some decisions about how you want to use them. You've got a roster full of great kids, and some are even starting to show promise as football players, but how do you decide what ones to play at what positions? For many coaches, the most obvious way to break up the team into positions is a simple look test: Big kids are linemen, small kids are cornerbacks and running backs, tall lanky kids are your wide receivers, and the kids with broad shoulders become linebackers.

It's actually not a bad way to go about things in the early stages of practice, as long as you are keeping an open mind. Just because one kid is fast does not necessarily mean he will make the best running back. Obviously speed is an advantage if used in the right way, but a different kid might turn out to be a very good inside runner despite the fact he is not very fast. By that same token, another kid might look like a receiver when in fact he has the perfect instincts to be a pulling left guard. Keep your eyes open, and use common sense. If a kid looks like a safety but plays like a linebacker, don't force it. Looks can be deceiving, especially at this age. You never know how puberty is going to affect these kids, so it's far too early to start making assumptions about what they will look like by the time they hit high school.

For the most part, the kids themselves are going to be happy just being out there running around playing football. For the majority of them, it won't really matter if they are playing wide receiver or defensive end; it's all the same to them. This is one of the many reasons why it's essential to rotate players through multiple positions. This will give you, the coach, a good look at your players working at different positions next to different teammates, which should help you decide where each kid fits best. It also keeps things more interesting for the kids because they get to try out new things in practice and maybe even find a position they really enjoy playing.

Every once in a while, however, you will run into a kid who has his heart set on playing a certain position. Maybe he wants to be a wide receiver because that is the position his older brother plays for the high school team, or maybe he has posters of Peyton Manning on his wall and wants to be just like his idol. If the skill set matches up with the desired position, it's no problem to let him play the position, but he'll have to understand that other players need the opportunity to play that position as well.

In other cases, you may run into a kid who really wants to play corner-back when it is obvious he is better suited to play offensive line. In this situation, do not discourage the player by telling him he isn't capable of playing the position. Remember, you don't know how he'll mature physically as he gets older. A better approach is to praise the child for having a passion to play that position while making it sound positive that you are going to give him a chance to learn other positions as well so he can develop into the best football player he is capable of becoming.

Last, but certainly not least, rotating players through positions will help keep most of the parents happy. No matter how fair you aim to be as a coach, there will always be the parent who thinks his or her child should be playing more or should be playing a more important position. By rotating kids through multiple positions, you will give these parents an opportunity to see their kids play the position they want while hopefully eliminating—or at the very least limiting—their opportunity to complain.

Creating Successful Practice Plans

Up until now, this book has truly been aimed at ensuring your survival. Your life may never be in danger as a youth football coach, but your sanity certainly can be if you don't have the right plan. Chances are your team will need to learn far too much in far too little time as the players prepare for a game that is only a week or two away. Your natural reaction will be to throw as much stuff at them as you can cram into a practice, but coaching young kids is as much about knowing how much to teach as it is knowing what to teach. Having a great practice doesn't always mean having the perfect practice plan, but it does mean having a plan. Things aren't always going to run smoothly down to the minute—that's the nature of coaching—but at least you will have direction and a goal for what needs to be accomplished, even if you don't get around to covering everything in your plan.

By now, things have started to settle down, and you've hopefully gotten to know your players a lot better than you did back on day one. You should have a better understanding of the strengths and weaknesses of your team, and you can begin to formulate some unofficial expectations in the back of your mind for just how successful this team can be on the field. One of the biggest challenges—even for the most experienced coaches—is keeping more than a dozen 5- to 10-year-olds focused for an extended period of time. How do you know when a drill has run its course for the day and it's time to move on to something else? In most cases, it should be pretty easy to read. Kids wear their emotions on their sleeves; so when you start to see glazed-over eyes or kids start to pay attention to anything but what you're trying to teach them, it's probably a good sign that they are ready for something else. Just don't confuse acting out with being ready to move on. Some kids will do whatever it takes to get attention, and that doesn't necessarily mean the drill is over.

The key to any successful practice starts with having a plan. There is no winging it when it comes to coaching youth football, unless you want the inmates running the asylum. Typically, practices should keep the same general flow because kids understand order and repetition, but it's also good to mix in some unexpected fun or completely scrap your practice plan every once in a while to keep things enjoyable. A standard practice should start with stretching, followed by a warm-up and drills before moving into skill instruction. Be sure to mix in humor and games, and give them something to look forward to at the end of practice, such as speed football or something else fun but also beneficial. If it's a really hot day, having a water balloon fight might help team morale, but having one every day won't make you a better football team.

Warm-Up and Stretching

It's no secret that stretching becomes more important as a person gets older, but even kids need to limber up before every workout. They are growing all the time and their young muscles need to be stretched out, especially considering they probably haven't been used for anything other than hide-and-seek and capture the flag. It might seem like a big chunk of time—especially if you are getting only 60 minutes for practice instead of 90—but you should allot 15 to 20 minutes for the warm-up. This is a big reason why it's important to make sure the kids show up on time for practice so you can get started right away. Even if there are some stragglers, you should go ahead and get the kids started on stretching while the others are still filtering in. This should also help you send a message to the parents that it's important to be on time. Figure 2.1 provides a sample warm-up routine you can use with your team.

If you have played organized football before—or any major sport, for that matter—then you have an idea of where to get started with a warm-up. Traditional sprinter stretches and jumping jacks are fine for the first day, but football stretching is about more than just limbering up, especially for kids this age. Although working on flexibility and avoiding injury are the primary goals of warming up, it's also good to incorporate as much actual football stuff into your warm-up as possible. This is all new to your players, and if they are going to learn to incorporate dynamic movement into their game, they need to practice it as much as possible. Using plyometrics is a great way to target the right muscles to produce fast, powerful movements that, over time, will help the kids run faster,

Figure 2.1   Sample Warm-Up Routine

Each activity should be performed for 30 seconds (in each direction or for each side as applicable) unless otherwise noted.

Activity*	Description
The Beat	This chant creates enthusiasm and team unity. The players clap their hands in unison. Then, the coach shouts *Are you ready?* twice. Each time the team responds, *Yes, sir!*
Jumping jacks	Players complete 10 jumping jacks in unison and count them aloud.
Arm circles	While standing, players make large arm circles with one arm, moving the arm forward at first and then to the back. Repeat with the other arm.
Neck circles	Players roll the head to the left, gradually and slowly completing a few full circles. Repeat with circles to the right.
Trunk rotations	Bending forward slightly at the waist, players circle the torso in a large circle to the left, leaning to the side, to the back, to the other side, and back to the front. Repeat with circles to the right.
Stretch it down	With feet about shoulder-width apart, players bend at the waist and stretch the hands down toward the feet.
Stretch it down with leg cross	Players cross the right foot in front of the left, then bend at the waist and stretch the hands down toward the feet. Repeat with the left leg crossed in front of the right.
Leg stretch	Players sit with the right leg extended in front of the body. The left leg should be bent at the knee, and the foot should rest near the side of the right thigh. Players lean the torso toward the right leg just far enough to feel a stretch in the back of the right leg. Repeat on the other side.
Shoot it through	While standing with feet a little wider than shoulder-width apart, players bend at the waist and reach the hands under the body and between the legs.
Hit its	While standing with feet a bit wider than shoulder-width apart, players shift their weight rapidly from one foot to the other. Each time the coach yells *Hit it!* the players drop their whole bodies to the ground and immediately get back up on their feet and continue the chopping motion with their legs. Players should show enthusiasm in this activity by cheering and yelling as they drop down and get back up.

Push-ups	Players move into a standard push-up position with the torso and legs extended straight out from the shoulders. Weight should be on the toes and hands. The coach counts aloud to 10, and on each count players complete a full push-up.
Crunches	While lying on the back with the feet flat on the floor and the knees bent, players cross the arms across the chest or place them behind the head to support (but not pull up on) the neck. The coach counts aloud, and on each count players lift the upper back off the ground, hold for a count, and then release back to the ground.
Neck isometrics	Players partner up. One player moves to his hands and knees. His partner stands near his head and provides resistance for these exercises: 1. The partner laces his hands under the player's chin. The player presses his head downward against the partner's hands. 2. The partner places his hands on the back of the player's head. The player presses up against the partner's hands. 3. The partner positions his right knee on the right side of the player's head. The player presses his head against the knee. 4. Same as step 3 but on the left side.
The Beat	Repeat the chant as previously explained.
Jumping jacks	Players complete another 10 jumping jacks, counting as before. Then, they sprint together to form a huddle.

*Players should jog to and from the various drill areas on the field.

jump higher, throw farther, and hit harder. Power skipping, repeated long jumps, alternate-leg bounding, repeated tuck jumps, single-leg hops, and squat jumps are all great exercises for increasing the force of muscle contractions, which will eventually increase an athlete's power output. Keep in mind that these are young kids, so keep the plyometric workouts low-intensity and low-volume.

The warm-up is also a good time to incorporate sprint work, backpedaling, and change of direction. These are all skills the kids will need in order to become good football players. Most young kids have never used their hips intentionally before, so have them do a warm-up such as carioca. This warm-up is performed by moving laterally, crossing the trailing foot in front of the lead foot, stepping with the lead foot, and then crossing the trailing foot behind the lead foot. Players should then repeat the movement in the other direction. Carioca gives players a chance to warm-up for defensive back moves, such as popping their hips in a backpedal or rotating their hips side to side like a defensive back. Another good thing to work on is explosive stretching exercises, such as standing long jumps (or Smurfs), and knee-bend exercises. Last, don't forget about those hamstrings, as football players are often prone to poor hamstring flexibility. We mentioned the sprinter stretches earlier, but other good hamstring exercises include the standing hamstring stretch, toe touches, and the sitting hamstring stretch. Frankensteins, in which players hold their hands straight out in front like Frankenstein and kick one leg at a time straight up in the air, attempting to touch the toes to the fingers of the opposite arm, are another good warm-up for the hamstrings.

Before we move on to the next portion of practice, here are some good areas to focus on during the warm-up:

- Explosive acceleration and increased sprinting speed
- Balance and lower body strength
- Body awareness (understanding where the parts of the body are and how to move them)
- Muscular balance and coordination with the brain
- Flexibility, especially in the hamstrings

Creating a Practice Plan

After 20 minutes of warming up, it's only natural that you're going to want to go straight into playing football; but don't be in too much of a hurry to put in plays. You may need to let the kids scrimmage for 10 minutes or so just so they get a chance to run around and release some of that energy, but you need to break down what you want to do. Build from the ground up. Kids see Adrian Peterson or Tom Brady on TV and think football is all about running, passing, and catching; it's your job to know better.

Take your time; don't try to teach everything at once. It's not going to be easy for all of these kids to understand right away what you're trying to teach them, so go slow to start with. This should not be a crash course. This is about building a foundation for their football futures. If you have only 60 minutes for practice instead of 90, you'll obviously have to scale things back so you can fit everything in. After the warm-up, break the team up (if possible) for drills. In chapters 3 and 4 of the book, we provide a list of 10 drills for each side of the ball that will help your players develop the skills they need to play this game successfully. Pick one or two drills for offense and one or two drills for defense, and focus on those. Watch carefully to make sure the players are picking up proper technique, because letting them execute the drills improperly can do more damage in the long run than not having them do the drills at all.

After the drills, bring the team together and work on the three main team phases of organized football: offense, defense, and special teams. At the higher levels, all three of these can be equally important, but at this level it is definitely more beneficial to focus on offense and defense. Figures 2.2 and 2.3 provide you with sample 90- and 120-minute practice plans.

Getting the Players Ready to Play

The end of practice is a good time to lay the groundwork for your offensive and defensive philosophy. It's still too early to start focusing on complex plays, but the kids should know what an offense and defense are supposed to look like. Teach terminology: Explain the difference between a linebacker and an offensive lineman so the kids will know what you're talking about when you tell Johnny to go play middle linebacker. Explain what it means to snap the ball or take a handoff, because many of the players on your team have never done either. Incorporate and explain terminology such as offside, holding, and facemask so that the kids become familiar with these football words that have no real meaning in the outside world. You want to think long term, but it's never too early to start teaching your players to think like a team.

Chapters 3 and 4 outline some valuable offensive and defensive drills that will help your players develop the skills they need to play competitively. There are also some smaller things you can do every day to help speed up the process. Have the kids practice throwing and catching the ball while on the run instead of standing still. Practice catching the ball and tucking it away to avoid fumbles, because even the most obvious lineman might end up playing fullback someday. Ball handling is another important skill that needs to be covered on a daily basis. Practice snapping the ball from center to quarterback along with taking handoffs. If a running back is taking a handoff to the right of the quarterback, his inside elbow should be up with his right arm on the bottom, forming a nice pocket for the quarterback to stick the ball.

No matter what position you think they will play, all the kids should handle the ball in practice and get a chance to throw and catch the ball. This will give you a chance to find out which of your kids are best suited

Figure 2.2   Sample 90-Minute Practice Plan

Duration	Skill or activity	Exercises or drills
5:00 to 5:01	Jumping jacks	Players complete 10 jumping jacks in unison and count them aloud.
5:01 to 5:10	Stretching	Players stretch arms, legs, shoulders, neck, and back. Refer to figure 2.1 on page 24.
Water break		
5:15 to 5:20	Offensive drill	Break team into different offensive positions and do stance and step drills. 1. Stance and Release drill (page 64) 2. Power Step drill (page 70) 3. Angle Step drill (page 71)
5:20 to 5:35	Team offense	Run plays and formations you will be using this week.
5:35 to 5:40	Team punt	Line up in punt formation, and do all punt plays including fakes. See chapter 7.
Water break		
5:45 to 5:50	Defensive drill	Perform drills that practice proper first step. 1. Explosive Step drill (page 95) 2. Man in the Mirror drill (page 97) 3. Angle Tackle drill (page 93)
5:50 to 6:05	Team defense	Full team vs. offensive plays you expect to face.
6:05 to 6:10	Punt return	Practice catching punts and returning. Work on all phases of punt return including punt blocking. See chapter 7.
6:10 to 6:20	Speed football	Play a large game of speed (or ultimate) football or something else fun (see page 18).
6:20 to 6:25	Conditioning	Run laps around the field, run up a hill, or do sprints across the field.
6:25 to 6:30	Team meeting	Go over the lessons of the day and upcoming practice and game schedules.

Figure 2.3　Sample 120-Minute Practice Plan

Duration	Skill or activity	Exercises or drills
5:00 to 5:01	Jumping jacks	Players complete 10 jumping jacks in unison and count them aloud.
5:01 to 5:10	Stretching	Players stretch arms, legs, shoulders, neck, and back. Refer to figure 2.1 on page 24.
Water break		
5:15 to 5:30	Offensive drill	Break team into different offensive positions and do stance and step drills. 1. Stance and Release drill (page 64) 2. Power Step drill (page 70) 3. Angle Step drill (page 71)
5:30 to 5:45	Team offense	Run plays and formations you will be using this week.
5:45 to 6:00	Defensive drill	Perform drills that practice proper first step: 1. Explosive Step drill (page 95) 2. Man in the Mirror drill (page 97) 3. Angle Tackle drill (page 93)
6:00 to 6:15	Team defense	Full team vs. offensive plays you expect to face.
6:15 to 6:25	Tackling	Work on proper tackling form (see page 76): head up, feet apart, hips low. Step into ballcarrier, head in front, and wrap up. No need to take player to the ground.
Water break		
6:30 to 6:35	Team punt	Line up in punt formation, and do all punt plays including fakes. See chapter 7.
6:35 to 6:40	Punt return	Practice catching punts and returning. Work on all phases of punt return including punt blocking. See chapter 7.
6:40 to 6:50	7 on 7	Run offense vs. defense in game setting without linemen or rushing (all passing).
6:50 to 6:55	Conditioning	Run laps around the field, run up a hill, or do sprints across the field.
6:55 to 7:00	Team meeting	Go over the lessons of the day and upcoming practice and game schedules.

for what. Remember, equal playing time is a must. If you are looking for a guide to winning games at all costs, then coaching youth football is not the place for you. Winning is nice, but it is far from the top priority when it comes to coaching kids this age. For your players, this is about learning to play the game the right way, which means for you it's about learning to teach the game the right way. Your kids will call you Coach, but you are also a teacher, and it's your job to give these kids life lessons along the way. It's our job to prepare you.

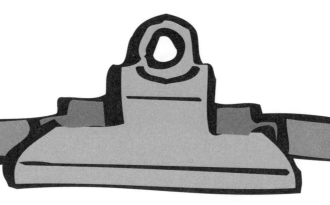

The Coach's Clipboard

✔ A coach is required to wear many different hats, so be ready for anything and remember to go with the flow.

✔ Keep the first few practices extremely simple.

✔ Learn every kid's name, even if it means writing their names on a piece of masking tape and sticking it across the front of their helmets.

✔ Keep an open mind when it comes to picking positions.

✔ Have practice planned down to the minute.

✔ The warm-up should focus on developing acceleration, speed, balance, lower body strength, and flexibility.

✔ Teach terminology every day so kids understand what you are telling them to do when you use football lingo.

✔ Every kid should handle the football, and every kid should get a chance to play every position.

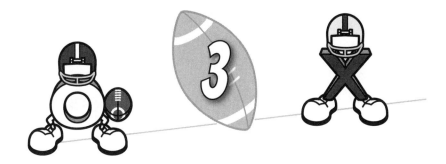

Developing Offensive Skills With 10 Simple Drills

Being a youth football coach is more about laying the groundwork—or planting the seed, if you will—for a player's future than it is about putting a finished product on the field. Teaching your players the very basics of the sport will give them the foundation they need to succeed at the higher levels. Although that should certainly be your primary concern at this level, it is also your job to put a team on the field that knows how to do more than just line up in the proper stance. You have to get the players moving in the right direction, and that means running an offense.

This can be a tricky endeavor with kids this young, but the 10 drills at the end of this chapter will not only help your players in the future but also allow you to put a team on the field that might just be able to score a little bit. Although many different things go into moving the football efficiently, a coach can begin to develop an effective offense by teaching the proper footwork and stances it takes to play any position on the football field at any level, as well as the ins and outs of four main position groups: quarterback, running back, wide receiver, and offensive line.

Offensive Stances, Footwork, and Technique

Great football players are built on a foundation of first-rate stances and exceptional footwork. The best way to begin any football position is to start with the two-point stance (see figure 3.1). This is where a player stands with his knees bent, butt down, and back straight. It's the kind of stance a running back or linebacker might use in the game, but it's invaluable for every player on the team, regardless of what position he eventually plays. Remember, you are going to be rotating players through multiple positions, so everyone should need to use this stance at one time or another. It is also much easier to transition from teaching a two-point stance to teaching a three-point stance than it is to explain the two stances independently. Most defensive stances are variations of the two-point stance, with the primary exception being the defensive line.

Once most of your players have started to understand the difference between a good stance and a bad one, the next step—literally—is working on footwork. Kids know how to run—they've been doing it their whole

Figure 3.1 Proper two-point stance.

lives—but they have no idea how to prepare for a tackle or what the proper footwork should be for a quarterback. You can actually give the players on your team more power in each tackle simply by encouraging them to keep their legs flexed and feet moving as they drive through a ballcarrier. A tackler should always keep his feet lined up under his shoulders to maintain proper body control and avoid overpursuit.

On offense, you should practice stance work with the offensive line. Have the players start in a three-point stance (see figure 3.2), and practice which foot they should start with first, depending on whether it's a running play or a passing play. In a three-point stance, the player should have one hand on the ground just inside his rear foot and just in front of his shoulders. His butt should be down, his back straight, and his chest out with the weight evenly distributed so he can explode forward without falling over.

It's important to teach these fundamentals at a young age, but it's still not time to give a lecture on proper footwork. Keep things fun, and keep the kids involved. Incorporate a cone drill using three or four cones into

Figure 3.2 Proper three-point stance for an offensive lineman.

your coaching, and have the kids work on using proper steps. Have them work on leading with the outside foot while moving side to side or front to back without looking down at their feet. They should keep their butts down and move on the balls of their feet instead of their heels. For more on footwork, see the drills dealing with footwork at the end of this chapter. If you have assistant coaches, break the kids into smaller groups, but either way, every kid should be involved in the drill.

Quarterbacks

There might not be a more important position in all of sports than the quarterback. It's like the lead singer of a band, the point guard of a basketball team, and the commanding officer of an army battalion all wrapped into one. Most kids are going to want to play quarterback because it seems glamorous. They see Tom Brady on TV and they think *sports star*, but not everyone is right for the position. It takes a leader, an athlete, an intellectual, and an extremely competitive spirit to play the position well.

We mentioned earlier that it's important for every kid to get a chance to play every position throughout the season, but quarterback is tricky because of how important the position is to everything you do on offense. The quarterback touches the ball on every single play, and let's face it,

Time to Huddle Up

Before your players can take the field on offense, don't forget to teach them how to huddle up. It might seem like a simple process to stand in a circle and go over the play call, but try getting 11 kids to do anything without practice and instead of that organized huddle you see on Sundays, you'll have a three-ring circus on your hands.

A good huddle starts with the center setting up 5 yards behind the ball and calling out a command word followed by the down and distance. This is important because your players will not understand the difference between first and 10 and third and 2 unless you make it a point to teach and reteach them. In some leagues, the coach will be allowed in the huddle to talk with the players and call the plays; in others the quarterback will be forced to remember the plays and call them out in the huddle. Find out the rules for your league.

Either way, no one should talk in the huddle except the person calling the play. That person gives the formation, play, and snap count. Be sure to go over the snap count three or four times just to make sure everyone is on the same page. All players should then break the huddle in unison on the command of the coach or quarterback and sprint to the line of scrimmage.

not every kid is going to be able to handle that responsibility. It's better to give every kid a chance to try playing quarterback in preseason practice before narrowing in on a much smaller group of players (say four or five) who will continue to get practice at the position throughout the season.

Gripping the Football

As you watch your players during the warm-up, you should start to get a sense for which ones might have a chance to play quarterback—although it's important to keep in mind how often your quarterback is actually going to be asked to throw the football more than 5 yards. Before you can really make a decision, however, every kid on the team should learn the proper way to grip the ball. Each passing grip will differ slightly from player to player depending on hand size. The smaller the hands, the more toward the middle they will need to grip the football, so you're going to want to start there and eventually have the kids with larger hands slide theirs farther back on the ball.

When learning the correct grip, quarterbacks should extend the index finger toward the tip of the football but just below the laces, with the thumb and index finger forming the letter C around the football (see figure 3.3a). The middle and ring fingers should touch the football, and the pinkie finger can rest on the laces (figure 3.3b). There should be some air between the ball and the palm of the hand. Ultimately, it's essential that the quarterback feels he has complete control of the ball. If it is slipping out of his hand like a water balloon, there is no way he's going to be able to throw it down the field.

Figure 3.3 When gripping the football correctly, (a) the thumb and index finger form a C around the ball and (b) the middle and ring fingers touch the ball and the pinkie finger rests on the laces.

Taking the Snap

Before your young quarterback can air it out for his first touchdown pass, it's important to get him in a position to throw, and that starts with the exchange from the center. There is more to having a good snap than just making sure the ball doesn't end up on the ground. The goal of every exchange on the snap when the quarterback is under center should be for the ball to come back to the quarterback in a position he would like to pass from. Young quarterbacks should learn early the importance of keeping their eyes downfield—while also having a feel for what's going on around them in the pocket—which means he should not be looking down at the ball to make sure the laces are in the proper position.

Before your young quarterbacks jump right into taking snaps from a center, they should practice the exchange with you or one of your assistants. From a kneeling position, the coach should hand the ball to the quarterback as if he is taking a snap so he gets comfortable with the feel of it. This will also give the coach an up-close look at the quarterback's hands to make sure he is using the proper grip. To teach quarterbacks how to properly take a snap, have them place their hands together with the bottom of their palms touching (see figure 3.4), the throwing hand on top. Hands should be spread open like a clam to make a pocket. The thumbs should be together, with the top thumb slid back about halfway down the bottom thumb so that the nail is between the two knuckles. This will help the kids keep their hands closer together to secure the football.

Keeping this hand position, the quarterback should bend his knees and place his hands under the center's butt in a manner that is comfortable—but not too familiar—for both players (see figure 3.5). Knowing kids, there will be a few in the bunch who think this is something gross—chalk that one up to having older brothers—so be prepared for some "ewws" and plenty of laughter. If you don't acknowledge it, the kids will typically let it go after a few minutes. When taking the snap, the quarterback should push up with the bottom hand while squeezing the football tightly.

One major variation of the quarterback–center exchange is the shotgun snap. Not many teams at this level will run plays out of the shotgun, but if they're doing it at the high school level in your area, then it might be a good idea to get the kids familiar with it. Running out of the shotgun means positioning the quarterback 3-4 yards behind the offensive line (see figure 3.6). The center will need to long snap the football in order to get it to the quarterback. The center should start in a good stance with his feet shoulder-width apart, his head up, butt down, and back straight. The ball should come through his legs with enough velocity to get to the quarterback, but not so much that it's hard for the quarterback to handle.

Figure 3.4   Proper hand placement for taking a snap.

Figure 3.5   Correct position for the center and quarterback during the snap.

Figure 3.6 Correct position for the center and quarterback during a long snap.

The center should be able to keep the snap straight and in a catchable area for the quarterback without having to look through his legs, because if he looks through them he will get blasted backwards by the defensive lineman across from him before he even looks up.

Dropping Back

Footwork is important for all players on a football team, but nowhere is it more critical than at the quarterback position. Before they begin the drop back, quarterbacks should have both hands firmly on the football as they take the snap, bringing it back to a throwing position while rotating the shoulders. Both hands should remain on the football, which will help young quarterbacks keep the front shoulder closed when they throw.

There are three main drop-back techniques depending on what type of pass the quarterback is going to throw. The first is a three-step drop back, which is used primarily for short, quick passes such as slants and curls. The second is a five-step drop back, which is used for intermediate passes such as deep in and out routes, and the third is a seven-step drop back used for deep passes such as fades and post routes. Unless you come across a kid during warm-up with the last name Marino, it's not likely you'll be using very many seven-step drops at this level because your kids won't have the arm strength to throw deep passes. However, kids should still learn the correct footwork at some point during the season because all three techniques are very similar.

A three-step drop should start with one long stride backward beginning with whichever foot is on the passing-arm side (see figure 3.7a)—meaning if your quarterback is right-handed, then his right foot should be the one going back first—followed by two short steps. The second step is a crossover step (figure 3.7b), and the final step is a plant step (figure 3.7c), which the quarterback will use to throw the ball. The five-step drop is very similar, except it starts with three long backward strides followed by two quick steps. The seven-step drop follows a similar pattern, as it requires five long backward strides followed by two quick steps, but the key is to have the legs crossing over on the second and fourth steps. The final step on each and every drop back should be the plant step to deliver the throw.

On a misdirection play, the quarterback will use a reverse out step where he pivots away from the line of scrimmage. That means opening with the right foot if he intends to go left. Make sure the quarterback is also hiding the football.

Figure 3.7 The three-step drop consists of (a) a long stride backward with the throwing-side foot, (b) a crossover step, and (c) a plant step.

Making a Textbook Pass

The first time your players attempt to make a pass, the ball's chances of going backward, sideways, or straight up in the air are just as good as its chances of actually going forward. Most kids have no idea when to release the ball or how to get it going in the direction they want. As a quarterback reaches his plant step on the drop back, the football should be at ear level and both hands should still be on the ball (see figure 3.8*a*). The player should then step forward with the opposite foot—if he's right-handed he should plant with his right foot and step with his left—in the direction he would like to throw the ball (figure 3.8*b*). It's important that the stepping foot is pointed at the target. The quarterback should propel the ball forward by applying pressure just behind the center point of the ball (figure 3.9*c*), moving the ball up over his head and then releasing it. Coaches should watch for elbow elevation and make sure players are pronating their wrists (a counterclockwise twist for the right forearm and a clockwise twist for the left). Quarterbacks should be rotating their shoulders on every throw.

As the ball is released from the hand, it should come off the pinkie finger first and then the ring finger and so on until finally it separates itself

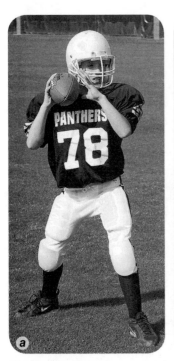

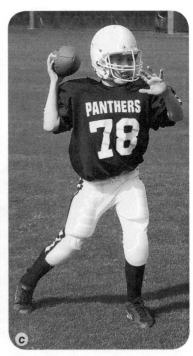

Figure 3.8   To make a pass, the quarterback (*a*) raises the ball to ear level on the drop step, (*b*) steps with the nonthrowing foot, and (*c*) propels the ball forward by applying pressure just behind the center point of the ball.

from the index finger. An easy—and funny—way to coach this technique is by telling the kids to "flick a booger" off their finger as they finish the throw. This might sound a little gross, but it will get a lot of laughs, and more important, it will teach the kids to let the ball go with the index finger and flip the wrist down as they finish their throws.

Whether it be intangibles such as leadership and poise or physical abilities such as throwing on the run or moving in the pocket, much more goes into being a great quarterback than just knowing how to pass. This, however, will lay the proper foundation for any players who go on to play quarterback at a higher level. Take your time; don't be in a hurry to teach them everything about passing all at once. Kids learn slowly, but what they come to understand at this age will last them a lifetime.

Making a Pitch

Another skill quarterbacks should have, especially in an offense that features option or sweep plays, is the ability to execute a proper pitch in order to get speedy running backs to the outside. A pitch is similar to the sweep play, but a pitch allows the running back to get wide in a hurry without having to come meet the quarterback to get the football (see figure 3.9).

On a pitch play, the quarterback should push the ball toward the running back, driving his thumb through the football while aiming for the numbers of the running back's jersey. There's nothing worse than shorting a pitch, so quarterbacks who are going to try it in a game should practice daily until they master the art of getting the football to the running back at his numbers.

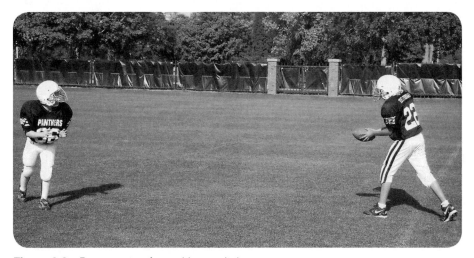

Figure 3.9 Proper setup for making a pitch.

Running Backs

No matter how good your passing attack may be—and at this level it's not a good idea to expect too much—every coach eventually learns the importance of a dependable running game. Some teams use a good running game to set up their passing attack, while others use their dynamic passing game to set up the run, but one way or another your team will need some balance.

Unlike quarterback, where you should begin to see two or three kids separate themselves from the group early in the season, running back is a position that can be played by almost anyone at this level. Obviously, some kids are going to be better than others, and there will be times where you want your best athlete carrying the ball, but it shouldn't be a one-man show. Every kid wants to have the ball in his hands, especially when the parents are watching, so share the wealth.

Taking the First Step

On the surface, it might seem as if running back is a position where you just give a kid the ball and get out of his way. Believe it or not, a lot of coaching goes into making a good running back, and it starts with a good first step. The difference a proper stance can make is especially true at running back, where the right starting point can help a player get off to a quick first step.

A running back should begin with his knees bent and his feet even at shoulder-width apart. A fullback will generally have one hand on the ground in a three-point stance, but a true tailback will be in a two-point stance with his hands on his thigh pads. The first step will be a quick, short step beginning with the outside foot (closest to the side of the field the play is directed to go) in the direction the running back is heading (see figure 3.10). (At this level, you want players to get their hands ready as quickly as possible to receive the ball, which is covered in the next section.) That means if the run play is going to the right, the back should step with his right foot first. He must be careful, however, not to tip his hand on which way the play is going by leaning or in any way signaling the defense. You can practice this with your team by having the players line up in the correct stance for a running back; call out a direction that the play is going (right or left), and have them practice their first couple steps so that you can analyze their technique and instruct where necessary.

Figure 3.10   A running back's first step should be a short and quick step with the outside foot in the direction he wants to go.

Securing the Handoff

Before your players can dance their way to the end zone, they first need to learn how to secure the football so they don't leave it lying on the field in the middle of their 30-yard cha-cha. They should learn the difference between taking a handoff and getting a pitch, because these are two very different things that require a unique set of skills. Toss plays are going to be significantly more difficult for kids at this level because of their small hands and the high level of eye–hand coordination involved. You may therefore want to limit the amount of pitch or option plays you run during games, but it's a good thing to practice if you have some extra time.

To produce a good handoff, both the quarterback and running back need to be on the same page, and they need to use proper footwork— there it is again—to make sure they meet in the right place at the right time for the exchange. As he prepares to take the handoff, the running back should form a pocket with his arms where the quarterback can stick the football (see figure 3.11). The inside elbow should be up, just below the shoulder, with the forearm extended across the chest. The outside arm (farthest away from the quarterback on the handoff) should be on the bottom, forming a basket along the lower abdomen. The quarterback should place the ball right in that pocket, and the running back should then secure the football with both hands—one over each end of the football (figure 3.12).

The handoff is an essential aspect of every offense at any level. If your team can't hand the football off without fumbling, your team is going to have a very hard time scoring points. There are not many demands you should make of your players at this level—they are kids, and mistakes are going to happen—but holding on to the football is one of the few. Your team should practice the exchange between the quarterback and running back from different angles and in different directions until everyone feels comfortable with both taking and giving a handoff.

Figure 3.11   Running back's pocket for receiving a handoff.

Figure 3.12   Running back securing the ball after a handoff.

Finding Daylight and Cutting

With enough practice, every player on your team—or at least most of them—should be able to learn the proper stance, footwork, and technique for taking a handoff. What will separate the good running backs from the rest is what they do with the ball once they have it in their hands. On each running play, there will be a designated gap through which the running back is supposed to carry the ball. The word *gap* is simply a way of quantifying the space between two offensive linemen so that a ballcarrier knows where he is supposed to go. The space between the center and the guard is commonly referred to as the *A gap*, the space between the guard and the tackle is called the *B gap*, the space between the tackle and a tight end is referred to as the *C gap,* and the space outside the tight end is the *D gap* (see figure 3.13). Knowing where the play is going and which gap he is supposed to run through will allow the running back to hit the hole with explosion. For the kids to understand which gap is

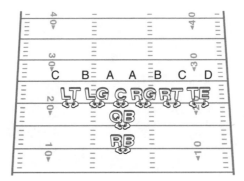

Figure 3.13 Running backs need to make their way through the A, B, or C gap.

which, they will need to see it with their own eyes. Demonstrate the different gaps in practice and possibly even send the players home with a diagram that has the appropriate labels.

Once a running back is able to hit the hole and come through on the other side, it's up to him to elude would-be tacklers. Speed and vision are two of the best tools a running back can possess, but not all of the kids on your team will be blessed with these assets. To help your players pick up more yardage, teach them how to break tackles and evade defenders. It might be a little early for the stiff arm or the spin move—although you can begin to gauge when some of the more talented players on the team are ready to add these weapons to their game—but a well-timed juke move (cut) at this level could be the difference between a 5-yard run and a 30-yard touchdown.

To them, a well-timed juke move is as simple as hitting the joystick to the right or left on their video game controllers, but it's a little tougher than that to make a real tackler miss. To make a cut to the right, the ballcarrier should step hard with his left foot to the outside of the defender (see figure 3.14*a*), shifting his weight to the left foot. His head and shoulders should also move quickly to the left to make the defender believe that's where he wants to go. Instead, the running back will take a quick step back to the right with his right foot and follow with his left as he hopefully renders the would-be tackler off balance (figure 3.14*b*). This is something that can be practiced with every player on the team using one ballcarrier and one defensive player in each drill. A ballcarrier should keep the ball tucked in his outside arm, and at a higher level, would even switch arms when reversing field. At this level, however, you just want your players to secure the ball and keep it tucked away until they are tackled.

Figure 3.14   The running back eludes the tackler by *(a)* faking in one direction and then *(b)* stepping and moving in the other direction.

Teaching Bonus Skills

For most coaches, this is as much teaching as you can throw at a running back at this level, and many times even up to the high school level. A running back's ability to carry the football, find the holes, and break tackles is his livelihood. If a player can do that successfully, he will have a future at the position. How much of a future will obviously depend a lot on the kid's athletic ability. In other words, you can't develop what's not there. That shouldn't influence the way you coach at this level because you're not in the business of guessing which kids are going to develop at an older age.

As a youth football coach, you should treat every kid the same, but one of the biggest ways to help a young running back get a leg up on the competition is by helping him develop some bonus skills. Pass blocking and catching passes out of the backfield are two very important skill sets that most running backs have to learn at the high school or even college level. Any back who learns to do these things effectively at a young age will have a huge advantage over the kids who are one-dimensional, not to mention the fact that having more well-rounded running backs will help your football team tremendously. This is another reason it's important for all your players to practice all the drills in this chapter. Instead of trying to teach the kids blocking and catching separately, it might be more beneficial to have them spend some time blocking with the offensive line (see page 54) and catching passes with the receivers (see next section).

Wide Receivers

Wide receiver is one of the easiest positions in football for young players to learn. On the surface, it is really nothing more than glorified backyard football. The quarterback hikes the ball, and it's the receiver's job to run around and get open until the ball comes his way. Then all he has to do is catch it, tuck it away, and head for the end zone. Seems pretty simple, right? As you probably already assumed, playing receiver is a little more complicated than that.

Knowing where to be is only half the battle for receivers; knowing when to be there is what separates the really good ones from the others. A quarterback and his receivers need to be on the same page if the offense is going to develop any kind of rhythm. The great quarterbacks don't wait until the receiver is already open to make the pass; they let the ball fly when the receiver is still partially covered in anticipation that he will be completely open by the time the ball reaches him. That puts the onus on the receiver to run the correct route so that he's where he is expected to be when the quarterback is expecting him to be there.

Start and Stance

The key to every good route is a proper start. Getting off the line is crucial for a wide receiver regardless of whether the play is a run or a pass. On passing plays, wide outs will obviously need to get a good release in order to get open, but getting off the line is also important on running plays because your receivers will need to engage the defenders across from them in run blocking. Ultimately it's important to teach your young receivers to come off the line the same way each and every play so that the defense cannot use their release as a tell for what the offense is going to do.

To get off the line quickly, a receiver should start with the correct stance. He should assume a two-point stance with the inside foot forward and the other offset behind it (see figure 3.15). There should be a slight bend in the knees, and the receiver's hands should either be on his hips or in front with the elbows bent in a ready position. The receiver should have his eyes forward or looking in at the ball since it might be difficult for a split end to hear the quarterback's cadence all the way out near the sideline. Repeating the same stance every time will help a wide receiver stay disciplined with the snap count and being onside. Upon the snap, the receiver should run directly at the defender across from him before making a cut. This will help keep the defender off balance because he is unsure of where the receiver is headed.

Figure 3.15   Correct two-point stance for a wide receiver.

Catch and Secure

Using the proper stance, getting a great release, and finding an open area in the defense are all important parts of playing the wide receiver position, but they won't mean a whole lot in the end if the wide out can't catch a cold. Playing catch and learning how to catch properly are two different things entirely. Catching a football is an art form that requires a variety of hand positions depending on the flight of the ball. There are two primary hand positions, one involving the thumbs together and the other involving the pinkies together. If the receiver is facing the quarterback and the ball is thrown at his jersey number or higher, he would want to catch the ball with his hands open and the tips of his thumbs touching or almost touching (see figure 3.16). The tips of his index fingers should also be touching or almost touching, with the rest of his fingers pointing up so that his hands form a diamond in the middle, which serves as an imaginary bull's-eye for the tip of the ball. It also creates a window through which the receiver should look to find the football. This will help young players maintain eye contact with the football until it reaches their hands.

When the ball is thrown below the belt or a receiver is attempting to make an over-the-shoulder catch, he should keep his pinkies close together with his fingers spread and relaxed (see figure 3.17). This is where the term *soft hands* comes into play. Instead of batting at the ball with his hands, a receiver should cushion the football and absorb the catch with partially bent elbows. The catch should be made with the fingers and not the palms. The receiver should attack the ball at its highest point and catch it with the hands extended away from the body.

Figure 3.16   Proper hand position for catching balls thrown at the jersey number or higher.

Figure 3.17 Proper hand position for catching a ball thrown below the jersey number or catching a ball over the shoulder.

Attacking the ball doesn't mean an absence of soft hands; it's more an attitude about fighting for the football when it's in the air. A receiver needs to have the mentality that it's his ball and no one else's.

Novice players will want to pin the ball to their chests with a basket catch, but this presents an unstable environment in which the ball can bounce directly off the shoulder pads or be jarred loose by a defender. By catching the ball away from the body, the receiver increases the distance between the defender and the ball, which helps prevent the defender from breaking up the pass. The space also allows the receiver to use his most valuable asset—his hands.

Once the receiver—or running back, for that matter—has made the catch, he must secure the football before taking off down the field. After watching the ball into his hands, a receiver should then tuck the ball away, locking one tip in his elbow while placing the fingers over the nose of the ball (see figure 3.18). He should carry it high and tight against the side of his pads by applying pressure with his hand, forearm, and elbow at the same time. This is something every player can master over time, so

Figure 3.18   Proper position for securing the ball.

it should always be practiced. Teach your players to tuck the ball away on every catch, even when they aren't working on wide receiver drills. With enough practice, this should become second nature to every player on your team.

Offensive Line

Working on the skill positions will be fun for both you and your players, but great teams are built from the inside out. Quarterback is widely considered to be the most important position on the football field, but if your team doesn't have an offensive line that can protect him and give the receivers time to get open, it won't matter how good your passing attack looks during seven-on-seven drills. It might sound like an oversimplification, but football games are won and lost in the trenches. Even at this level, the team that can block for the run and the pass will probably be the one that comes out on top. At the college and pro level, the blocking schemes can be remarkably complex, but the key to coaching young kids how to play the offensive line—as with most other things—is to keep things simple. Develop a straightforward blocking scheme and stick with it. If you can get your players to do one thing well, you've accomplished more than you could know.

Most kids are not going to want to play offensive line when they first start out—which is yet another reason it's important to rotate your players through multiple positions—and who could blame them. There is no glory in playing on the offensive line, as the group is often underappreciated for the work they do. Outside of the center, offensive linemen don't get to touch the football, so it is easy for kids to feel as if they aren't really involved in the play. One way to circumvent this problem is to glorify the position during practice. Let the players know how important the offensive line is to a team's success, and make it a point to single these players out for praise when they make a good block. Getting kids excited about playing on the offensive line is more than half the battle.

Examining the Offensive Line

There are three primary positions on the offensive line (guard, center, tackle) that account for the five regular players up front; one secondary position, called the tight end, acts as an extension of the offensive line. Tight ends are used in more traditional formations (such as the I-formation), and they are typically quicker, more agile players who can both block and catch. Oftentimes, great blocking tight ends will turn into outstanding offensive tackles down the road, much like former Wisconsin All-American and current Cleveland Brown All-Pro left tackle Joe Thomas.

Tackles are the two outside players—or bookends—on the offensive line. They are typically your best pass protectors because they will often face the opposing team's best pass rushing defensive ends. At the higher levels, the best offensive tackles will have long arms and good athleticism, but at this level you should feel good about finding two kids who can stay on their feet consistently and keep their bodies between the defenders and the quarterback.

Inside the tackles are the two guards. These are typically your bigger, stronger run blockers who can move the line of scrimmage by pushing their defender backward. If you plan to use a lot of trap plays or sweeps (see chapter 5), you will need at least one guard who excels at pulling. That means he needs to be athletic enough to get out of his three-point stance and get down the line to the hole before the tailback does, but also tough enough to knock someone out of the way when he gets there. A good pulling guard should turn his back on the center by rotating his torso toward the side of the play. He should step flat and plant his foot hard downfield in the direction he is pulling. The guard needs to get down the line quickly and into the hole while maintaining good balance so he is ready for contact.

In the middle of the offensive line is the center, who acts like a glorified guard. The center is the only player besides the quarterback who touches the ball on every play, so ideally you would like to find a kid with his wits about him. It's important that a center and quarterback develop some chemistry for the snap because the last thing you want is the ball hitting the ground on the exchange.

Ready, Set, Block

As with most other positions, offensive linemen must be built from the ground up. Pass blocking and run blocking require two different types of footwork, and players need to become proficient at both if they want to have success on the offensive line. Using "ready" and "set" positions is a good way of teaching players the exact motion by setting up the final stance with an interim stance. In a ready position, the offensive linemen should line up in a two-point stance with their legs about a foot (.3 m) back from the line of scrimmage (see figure 3.19a). The eyes should look straight ahead, the feet should be slightly wider than shoulder width, and the toes should be pointed forward with the knees bent, chest out, and shoulders back. Upon the quarterback's command, all five linemen will snap into the set position by dropping into a three-point stance (figure 3.19b). Once a lineman is in the set position, he must stay frozen until the ball is snapped.

On run plays, an offensive lineman should explode off the football and make contact with the defender across from him as he attempts to push him back and out of the play to open a hole for his running back. Kids are not strong enough to do the kind of blocking you see on TV, so have them work on shoulder blocking. This might seem old-fashioned, but kids this age are more effective using this technique. The offensive lineman should pop the defender's shoulder pads with his hands—this is often referred to as *punching*, but you probably want to stay away from using that terminology with this age group unless you want a UFC fight breaking out in the middle of football practice. Instead, refer to it as *popping the pads* so players understand there needs to be some force behind it, along with the noise it should make (see figure 3.20). The hands must stay inside to avoid being flagged for holding, and the player should focus on getting under the opponent's center of force while driving his legs all the way through the whistle. This last part is what separates the great linemen from the rest.

Like many other positions in football, proper footwork is critical to the offensive line. Improper footwork can render a player ineffective. Two important steps for offensive linemen are angle steps and pull steps. On most plays, the first step should be with the play-side foot. On a run to the right, all five offensive linemen should work on stepping with their

Figure 3.19 Proper (*a*) ready and (*b*) set positions for offensive linemen.

right foot on an angle (angle step). Have them reach out with their hands and engage a defender as they step through. Pull steps should be flat and near to the ground because it's important to get moving in a hurry. If a pulling guard doesn't get to his hole before the running back, the whole play is blown up.

Figure 3.20   Correct technique for popping the pads.

Blocking Assignments

Teaching proper technique on the offensive line will help your team in ways you never imagined. It is surely the best way to help your players develop the fundamental skills they will need to play the position at a higher level, but it is actually not the most important thing when it comes to getting your young linemen ready for advancement. One of the most neglected areas in youth football is teaching kids whom to block. A lineman can perform a perfectly executed block using all of your teaching points, but if it is on the wrong player, someone is going to come through into your team's backfield unblocked. Conversely, performing a poorly executed block on the right player should be enough at this level to give your back enough room to pick up at least a few yards. That's why it is important to devote time during every practice to making running plays over and over again until all the players—especially the offensive linemen—know where they are supposed to be and whom they are supposed to block.

Drill 1 Taking the Snap

EQUIPMENT   1 football for every 2 players

PURPOSE   Teaching players the traditional exchange of the ball between quarterback and center, allowing them to get a feel for the physical part of it

PROCEDURE   Have your players pair off. For each pair, one player is the center and the other is the quarterback. Have the players practice taking snaps under center for five minutes, with the quarterback getting the ball cleanly. Start by having each pair snap the ball on the coach's signal (probably best to stick with using *Hike!*). As players get the hang of the drill, the partner playing center can try snapping the ball on each individual quarterback's command. Repeat the drill with the partners switching roles so that both players get a complete feel for the process.

COACHING POINTS   Watch the placement of the ball to make sure the center is snapping it in a way that it comes into the hands of the quarterback ready to be thrown. Teach communication between the center and the quarterback, and make sure the ball does not end up on the ground. That may happen in practice, but the goal of this drill is that it won't happen in a game. As noted, every player should get a chance to do both, but you may want your players vying to be the starting quarterback spending most of their time receiving the snap, and vice versa for players who are likely candidates to play the center position.

MODIFICATIONS   Do the same thing only out of the shotgun. Even if you don't intend to use much shotgun in your offense, this is a good way for young quarterbacks to get used to the feel of the ball. It's also a good way to identify long snappers, who can be in high demand. Many long snappers have been quarterbacks, so make sure the players are getting an opportunity to play both positions. Teach the two-hand snap as if it's a pass underneath the legs.

Drill 2 Partner Passing

EQUIPMENT   1 football for every 2 players

PURPOSE   Teaching quarterbacks to use proper wrist, elbow, and shoulder technique when throwing the ball (this drill also works well as a warm-up for all players at the beginning of practice)

PROCEDURE   Form two lines of players facing each other. The players in each line should kneel on one knee. The knee on the nonthrowing side should be forward with the foot flat on the ground, while the knee on the side of the throwing arm should be down on the ground. So, right-handed players will have the right knee on the ground and vice versa for left-handed players. Players should practice throwing from one knee to their partners in the other line. Continue the drill until every player has made 10 to 15 throws.

COACHING POINTS   Players should keep their thumbs under the ball and space out their fingers to apply pressure at five different points. The shoulders should be turned back to start, and the players should rotate their shoulders through on every pass. Watch for elbow elevation, and make sure players are pronating their wrists (counterclockwise twist for the right forearm and clockwise twist for the left).

MODIFICATIONS   To make the drill more competitive and more challenging, change the distance between partners. Have each partner take a step back after completing three passes in a row. Maybe start the more advanced passers in your group farther away from their partners (which means you will need to pair them with other kids who are more advanced). Or have them stand up (instead of kneeling) and practice the same techniques while putting their nonthrowing-side foot forward (instead of the knee).

Drill 3 Quarterback Footwork

EQUIPMENT   1 football for every player (but the drill can also be done without a football)

PURPOSE   Teaching proper footwork for a quarterback (since the footwork for all positions in football is comparable, this drill can be used to help all players improve their footwork)

PROCEDURE   Line up players side by side in one line, facing one direction. (If you have an assistant coach or a parent available, you may find the best approach is to have half the team do this drill while the other players focus on another drill.) Players start in a presnap position and work primarily on three-step drops. A right-handed quarterback should take a flat step to his right and drop his foot back behind to get as much depth as possible on each step. The left foot will then cross over the right before the player drops the foot, planting it for the throw. The pattern for left-handed players is the opposite. The entire process should cover 2 to 4 yards. You should start by facing the same direction as the players and modeling the steps, and then you should face the entire team and watch them run the drill after calling out a command such as *Ready, fire* or *set, go*. Then walk around and work with individual players on their technique.

COACHING POINTS   Watch to make sure the players are not wasting any steps. A long first step doesn't do much good if the second one is short. Look for a 45-degree angle on the turn step, and teach players to cover as much ground as possible in each step without losing balance. At the end of the drop, players should maintain good body position and be ready to throw.

MODIFICATIONS   Five- and seven-step drops can easily be built off a three-step drop once a player understands the footwork; just add two more for five-step drops and four more for seven-step drops. Another option is to practice the reverse step quarterbacks use on a misdirection play. There's no need to have the entire team work on this variation of the drill, so have only players who could actually play quarterback work on this modification separately.

Drill 4 Stance and Release

EQUIPMENT   None

PURPOSE   Teaching running backs stance and footwork; teaching receivers the proper technique for a release

PROCEDURE   Split the team into two groups. Have one group work as receivers in one area of the field and the other group work as running backs in another area of the field. If you're lucky enough to have the extra help, you can have an assistant or parent run the drill for each group so you can move between the two. Because of the similarities between receivers and running backs and the athletes who play the positions, switch the two groups after 5 or 10 minutes so players get to work on both positions.

The running backs (*a*) work on stance and footwork. If you have more than 10 kids in this group, split them into three or four small groups and have the groups take turns. If you have fewer, they can all do the drill together. Have the running backs line up 7 yards off the ball so they get used to the distance. The coach acts as the quarterback, giving the running backs the direction of the play so they can practice the proper footwork. If the play is going to the right, the running backs take their first steps with the right foot, but it's important they not tip off the defense as to which direction the play is headed. That means using the same stance on every play.

The receivers (*b*) practice getting an outside release. Pair up the players. One partner is the receiver and the other is a defender. If you have more than 10 kids, split them into a few small groups and have the groups take turns. The coach should signal the start of the drill by blowing his whistle or giving a command.

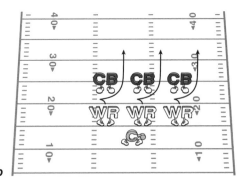

a   b

COACHING POINTS   Kids are creatures of habit. The more they do reps properly, the better their stance will get throughout the course of the season. If a kid is leading with his inside foot (running to the right, stepping with the left), make sure to correct him. It might not seem like a big deal if he's getting the handoff and hitting the hole, but eventually it will be, and this is about teaching fundamentals the right way. The same goes for receivers. They should be leading with the outside foot when trying to get an outside release. Additionally, during the drill, the defense is going to want to narrow the field by forcing the receiver inside, but it's important to use the entire field, sideline to sideline.

Drill 5 Cutting

EQUIPMENT Cones or bags; 1 football for every running back

PURPOSE Teaching running backs how to use cuts to make tacklers miss; teaching receivers how to use cuts to get open

PROCEDURE Split the team into two groups; have one group work as receivers in one area of the field and the other group work as running backs in another area of the field. If you're lucky enough to have the extra help, you can have an assistant or parent run the drill for each group so you can move between the two. For the running back group (*a*), set up cones or bags to represent the entire offensive line (or at least one side of it). Leave enough space between the cones or bags to represent the different gaps where run plays could be designed to go. Switch the two groups after 5 or 10 minutes so players get experience at both positions.

The receivers (*b*) practice getting in and out of cuts on their routes. Two players will be in the drill at one time. Have one player act as the defender and the other as a receiver. They should practice running directly at the defender before cutting off the outside foot to make a move inside. Their goal is to work on getting open. Running backs start with the ball in their hands or take a handoff from the coach and then find the appropriate hole, which teaches the backs to run toward daylight. Have one player act as the running back and another as defender. Change the hole as the drill progresses. They should only do subtle cuts in the hole, but the key to being a good running back is the ability to make defenders miss while holding on to the ball.

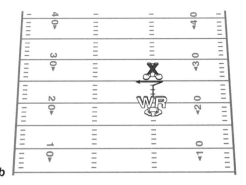

a   b

COACHING POINTS Watch to make sure the running backs and receivers are cutting off the outside foot (if they are going right they should plant with the left foot). If they cut off the inside foot, they will probably fall down. Talk to them about using the helmet and upper body to sell the fake, but they should never use the ball for that purpose. They should always hold the ball tightly against the rib cage with pressure from the elbow. They should use their fingers to cover the top or else the ball will fly out when they go to make their cuts. For the receivers, teach them to spring hard off the line directly at the defender across from them before making their cut to get open.

MODIFICATIONS For running backs who pick up on the cut more quickly, you can also teach them the spin move, which involves planting on the outside foot before spinning back to the inside.

Drill 6 Bad Ball

EQUIPMENT 1 football for every 2 players

PURPOSE Teaching players to catch passes that are not perfect spirals (this drill is also good practice for defensive players, who also need to practice catching bad balls)

PROCEDURE Pair up your players, and have them spread out in two long lines facing each other so the partners don't interfere with each other. Have the receivers throw passes back and forth. The goal should be to throw the ball as poorly as possible so the other player gets used to catching bad balls. This might mean just throwing wobbly passes but also could include intentionally throwing away from the receiver, as long as there is enough room. Each partner should catch 10 to 12 balls.

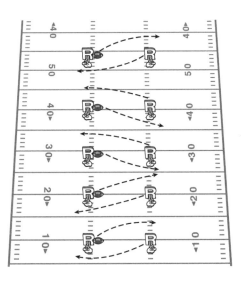

COACHING POINTS Make sure the players are catching the ball with the hands and not the chest. Balls that hit the shoulder pads will bounce free, so it's important to catch the ball with the hands away from the body. Teach the players to catch the ball and immediately tuck it away under the arm.

MODIFICATIONS This drill can also be used to work on the option pitch along with the sweep or toss running play covered in chapter 5. Have the backs practice catching poorly pitched balls with their hands and then tucking the ball away.

Drill 7 One-Hand Catch

🏈🏈 **INTERMEDIATE** *(Receivers)*

EQUIPMENT   1 ball for every coach; 2 cones

PURPOSE   Teaching the concentration and eye–hand coordination needed to play receiver

PROCEDURE   Set up two cones about 20 yards apart. Have the players line up in a single line at one of the cones. (If you have an assistant coach or parent helpers, you can set up two or three lines.) The coach lines up about 5 yards away from the center of the distance between the cones. The first player in line begins to move to his left (toward the other cone), and the coach throws a soft pass to the player's right. The player catches the pass with only his right arm, securing the ball between his hand and his biceps. After the catch, the player tosses the ball back to the coach and moves to the other cone, forming a new line. When all the players are in the new line, the drill is reversed. Players move through the new line, catching the ball with the left hand only.

COACHING POINTS   Watch the players' eyes to make sure they are looking the ball all the way into the hand. Make sure they are tucking the ball away, and don't be afraid to have them do it again and again until they start to get the hang of it. Because they are catching with one hand, they likely won't feel as bad about dropping the ball.

MODIFICATION   You can also use this drill for running backs with catching pitches or tosses.

Drill 8 Power Step

EQUIPMENT   1 or more blocking bags

PURPOSE   Teaching offensive linemen how to take short, powerful steps while maintaining balance; helping kids understand what it feels like to be in contact with a bag (or person) and what it feels like to have their hips in contact with a bag (or person).

PROCEDURE   Set up blocking bags or sleds along one of the yardage lines or in an open area. Have your players make even lines behind the blocking bags, and have them work on bending their hips in a good athletic stance on your command. Get them to practice taking short, powerful steps similar to a sumo wrestler before engaging the bag.

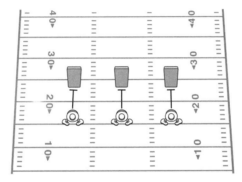

COACHING POINTS   Be sure players keep their heads up and backs straight as they prepare for contact. Watch to make sure the players are bending properly at the knees. Low man wins on the line, so standing straight up will not get the job done. Proper stance is the most important thing for the players to practice, but also make sure they are moving their feet. Look to see that they have a low center of gravity and good balance so they don't slide off the defender.

MODIFICATIONS   If you don't have blocking bags, you can pair up your players. The partners should face each other and put their hands on each other's shoulders, using each other for resistance. Have the partners engage simultaneously so they can get a feel for what it's like to have resistance on their bodies.

Drill 9 Angle Step

EQUIPMENT   None

PURPOSE   Teaching offensive linemen to lead with the proper foot when engaging a defensive lineman

PROCEDURE   Set up a mock offensive line with five players across the front (one center, two guards, and two tackles) and a defensive line right across from them. Have the offensive linemen practice stepping with the play-side foot at an angle and push the defenders back one step. (If it's a run to the right, all five offensive linemen should work on stepping with the right foot on an angle.) The defender is there to allow the offensive linemen to get a feel for making contact, so the defenders should allow themselves to be moved without resistance. The first time you do the drill, run it without the defensive line, but have the offensive linemen reach out with their hands as if to engage a defender as they step through. After that, you can run it with the defense in place. Keep running the drill until players get the footwork.

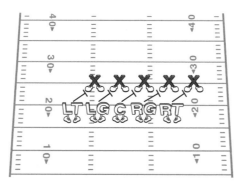

COACHING POINTS   Watch the players' footwork. If kids are still stepping with the wrong foot and you don't make them change that, it's going to be a lot harder to correct down the road. Again, watch their technique, and make sure they are playing low. If a player is standing up, don't hesitate to get right in there and show that you can get even lower. Just don't throw out your back!

Drill 10 Pull Step

EQUIPMENT 1 or more blocking bags

PURPOSE If you're going to run the trap play, you will need to teach your offensive lineman how to pull, and that starts with the proper footwork.

PROCEDURE Have five players line up to create an offensive line (two tackles, two guards, and one center). Much like the angle step, if a lineman is going to pull, he should step first with the foot on the same side to which he will pull. (If he's going to pull to the left, he should step first with his left foot.) Hold a blocking bag where a defender would be, and have the player use a pull step and hit the bag with the pull-side hand and shoulder. (You can also substitute an actual defender instead of a bag.)

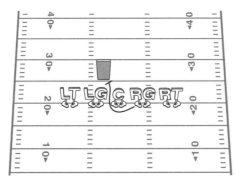

COACHING POINTS Keep an eye on the players' technique and footwork. Watch to make sure players are stepping with the correct foot as well as bending at the hips and staying low.

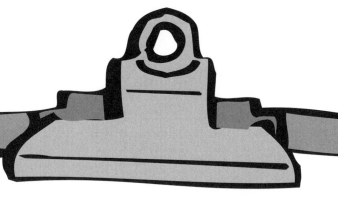

The Coach's Clipboard

✔ Great football players are built on a foundation of first-rate stances and exceptional footwork.

✔ The center should typically huddle the offense 5 yards behind the ball before every offensive play.

✔ Quarterbacks at this level will primarily use three-step drops.

✔ When quarterbacks reach their plant step, they should point the opposite foot in the direction of the receiver.

✔ As the ball is released from the hand, it should come off the pinkie finger first and then the ring finger and so on until finally it separates itself from the index finger.

✔ A running back's first step should be a short and quick step with the outside foot in the direction he wants to go.

✔ The running back eludes the tackler by faking in one direction and then stepping and moving in the other direction.

✔ Receivers should catch balls thrown at the jersey number or higher with the thumbs together, and they should catch balls thrown below the jersey number with the pinkie fingers together.

Developing Defensive Skills With 10 Simple Drills

Offense may sell tickets, but defense wins championships is a coaching mantra that has been around in every sport ostensibly since the dawn of time, or at least organized athletic competition. It speaks to the notion that a high-powered offense might be fun to watch, but a shutdown defense will help your team stay in the game even when things aren't clicking offensively. There won't be any tickets sold for your games unless you have a Jonas Brother on your team and a great marketing plan, but the cliché holds true for youth football.

Points are frequently hard to come by at this level. The final scores of youth football games can often look more like those of high-scoring baseball games. Depending on the talent in your league, some teams, through turnovers and penalties, will hold themselves to under 10 points, but that is certainly not true of all teams you will face. Teaching your players the fundamentals of tackling, getting penetration on the defensive line, playing in space, and defending the pass will give your team the essentials it takes to slow down a potent offense. Great defenses aren't built overnight, but teaching kids where to be and how to get there will put them in position to make plays consistently on the defensive side of the football.

The defense has one main priority on every play: Keep the other team out of the end zone. There are many smaller goals that defenses should attempt to accomplish along the way, such as sacking the quarterback, creating a turnover, and forcing a punt, but all of those take a backseat to stopping a touchdown. No matter how many yards a team gives up on any given drive, if the players keep the other team from scoring points, they have won that battle. This is often easier said than done, however, because one mistake by a key player on defense can free an offensive player for a touchdown. This is why it is so important to build a sound defense with 11 players working together.

Tackling

Every player on your football team, big or small, must learn the proper way to tackle. Without tackling, you're just playing glorified rugby. Whether a player is going to end up a defensive tackle, linebacker, or even cornerback, he must master the correct technique for taking down a ballcarrier. Using a proper form tackle will help your young players prevent neck injuries—which is always the number one priority for a coach at any level—but it will also make you a better football team. No matter how athletic your players are, a defense is only as strong as its ability to tackle. Teaching players the proper tackling technique at a young age is something that will stick with each kid throughout his playing career.

Some coaches believe that running a full-contact practice where players fly around crushing each other is the best way to prepare them for what it takes to play the game competitively. You want your players to be tough, but this is certainly not the age to have them beating each other into the ground as if it's the National Football League. Besides, practice time is extremely valuable and should be used primarily for teaching technique and assignments. Kids will pick up the physicality of the game as they go along.

Like many things in football, the proper form tackle starts with the right stance. A defender in the ready position should start with his knees bent, back straight, and head forward (see figure 4.1). His arms should be out in front, and he should stand on the balls of his feet, ready to launch in whatever direction the ball goes. Teach your players to mirror the ballcarrier and initiate contact by attacking the play rather than waiting back and catching the ballcarrier on his heels. Defenders should break down at the point of attack by bending their knees, sinking their hips, and arching their backs while keeping their eyes up (figure 4.2). Hits should be made number on number, with the defender's helmet to the

Figure 4.1   Proper ready position for a tackle.

Figure 4.2   Proper break down position.

side of the ballcarrier (figure 4.3). The helmet should never be used as a weapon—for the safety of both players—and a player should avoid dropping his eyes or placing his head in the middle of a ballcarrier's pads.

One of the most important aspects of tackling is the ability to wrap up. Players can hit as hard as they want, but good ballcarriers will break through arm tackles and bounce off shoulders. The only real way to make certain that a ballcarrier goes down to the ground is to wrap up. Make sure your players wrap their arms around the ballcarrier at the point of contact while lifting from the ground up as shown in figure 4.4. The hips should thrust forward and drive through the ballcarrier to create lift from the ground, while the legs continue to drive all the way through the tackle until the ballcarrier is on the ground or out of bounds.

Tackling drills such as the ones provided in this chapter will help your players practice the repetitive motion it takes to train their muscles how

Figure 4.3   Proper position for a tackle.

to make the proper form tackle every time. Use these drills every day (or at least every practice), and repeat them until proper tackling technique becomes second nature. In most cases, you want to praise your players for giving 100 percent effort even if they aren't doing things exactly the right way. This is not one of those cases. Compliment players for putting forth an effort during drills, but it's important to correct them when their form is off. Make sure each child knows whether he is doing it the right way or whether he still needs to work on his technique—his safety may very well depend on it.

While instructing your kids on the proper technique of form tackling, keep in mind what you are actually teaching them. The kids should learn how to do things the right way during drills, but how many times have you seen a perfect form tackle executed in a high school, college, or pro football game? During games, players should aim to use what they've

Figure 4.4   Technique for wrapping up a tackle.

learned about tackling, but things are usually moving much too fast for defenders to break down completely while lining up for the perfect number-on-number form tackle.

During drills, players are typically going one on one against a ballcarrier who is running right at them. On the field, things can quickly turn to chaos. A defender might have to fight through two or three blockers to get at the ballcarrier; in these circumstances, the defender is just trying to do anything and everything he can to make the stop. Sometimes that means forming up for a perfect tackle, but often that means hurling his body at the ballcarrier, grabbing on to something, and not letting go until the whistle blows. Educating your kids on the proper tackling technique will help them avoid neck and shoulder injuries while teaching them to wrap up and run through the ballcarrier, but don't be alarmed if you aren't seeing many perfect form tackles on game day. Just finding a way to keep the guy with the ball from crossing the goal line should be considered a victory on every drive.

It's also important to teach your players about angles. A ballcarrier's current location is not where he will be by the time the defender closes in on him. Kids at this age don't have a great understanding of time, distance, and speed, so teach them to take the right pursuit angles. Aim for where the player is going to be, not where he is right now. This might seem like a simple concept, but it can be rather complex for kids just learning about how to move their own bodies.

Defensive Line

Much like the offensive side of the ball, great defenses are built from the inside out. Having a defensive line that can penetrate the gaps against the run and pressure the quarterback in passing situations will make everyone else on the defense that much better. It can also make up for a lot of inefficiencies in other areas of the defense. There may not be a lot of complex blitzing at this level, but your back seven (linebackers and defensive backs) will feed off the play of your defensive front. If your defensive ends can put pressure on the opposing quarterback, his receivers won't have as long to get open, which means your cornerbacks won't have to cover as long. Along the same line, if your defensive tackles can keep opposing offensive linemen off your linebackers, it will free them up to make more tackles in the open field.

It would be easy to tell you that knowing the importance of having a good defensive line is half the battle, but this is not meant to be a book of fairy tales. Finding a dominating defensive line at any level can be one of the toughest tasks in football. Teams that do tend to be the ones that have the most success defensively—just ask the 2007 New York Giants. Fortunately, all is not lost if you don't happen to find a young Dwight Freeney on your roster. The teams you coach won't be going up against the likes of the Cowboys and Patriots, at least not the ones that play on Sundays.

Defensive Tackles

Depending on what type of defense you are going to run, there could be as many as three defensive tackles consistently on the field together or as few as one. A defensive scheme with three tackles, two ends, and two linebackers is called a 5-2; a scheme with one tackle, two ends, and four linebackers is most often referred to as a 3-4 look. These are examples of two schemes used at the high school, college, and pro levels, but you will probably want to stick with the typical 4-3 scheme that features two defensive tackles, two ends, and three linebackers.

Preferably, you will be able to put two big, strong athletes inside as your defensive tackles so they can create havoc and take up space. Over the years, this position has notoriously become one of the toughest spots to fill with talented players, if not the toughest. Even coaches at the high school and college levels struggle to find dominant defensive tackles to build their teams around, so don't lose any sleep at night if you don't happen to have two powerfully built athletes on the roster to plug in at the defensive tackle spots. Even if you are lucky enough to have a couple of beasts to put at defensive tackle, technique and assignment continue to be the most important things at this level.

A defensive tackle should begin in a three-point stance very similar to that of a blocker, except that his weight should be significantly more forward than a lineman on offense (see figure 4.5). The back is

Figure 4.5   Three-point stance for a defensive tackle.

still straight, hips are bent, and eyes are forward. Feet should be a little wider than shoulder-width apart, with the toes pointed slightly out to ensure balance and power. The player's weight should be on the balls of his feet, and some larger players may feel more comfortable setting one foot slightly behind the other. This will help them create more momentum going forward.

One hand should be on the ground with either the knuckles or fingers down, just inside the player's rear foot and just in front of the player's shoulders. This will allow the player to put weight on his hand, which will create forward momentum when the ball is snapped. Make sure your players know that not all of their weight will be on this hand; most of their weight should remain on the balls of their feet to keep them from toppling over or collapsing under the weight of their own bodies. The hand not being used in the three-point stance should either rest on the thigh pad or be up in an attack position where it can easily be used for a rip or swim move. For the rip move, a defender drives his arm up and under the near arm of the blocker to pin the blocker's arm. If the defender is moving to the left, the defender should hook his right arm under the right shoulder of the blocker. A swim move is similar but the defender uses his inside arm over the top of the blocker's shoulder like a freestyle swim move.

Having a player set up in the correct stance and shift his weight forward helps him get off the ball as quickly as possible. Defensive tackles are close enough to the ball that they can see when it is snapped, and they should explode off the line and into the backfield while staying low and keeping good balance. Much like an offensive lineman, defensive tackles must focus on staying low and getting under the blocker's pads (see player pictured on the right in figure 4.6). That means bending at the hips, keeping a low center of gravity, driving forward, and not popping straight up out of a three-point stance. You should run drills for both sides of the line that focus on the low man's winning the battle, because that is a critical aspect of what it takes to play in the trenches.

Defensive linemen should line up close to the neutral zone, which is a 2- to 3-foot (.6 to .9 m) restricted area around the football, but not inside it or they will be flagged for offside. As the players closest to the ball, tackles should keep their eyes forward searching for tells on the offensive line or in the backfield. If an offensive lineman has one foot slightly behind the other, it might tell the defense that the play is going to be a pass rather than a run. If a running back is leaning to one direction, there is a good chance he is accidently tipping not only that the play will be a run, but also to which side it is designed to go.

Figure 4.6   Defensive tackles must stay low and get under a blocker's pads.

Defensive Ends

Although most coaches will tell you that having dominant defensive tackles is the foundation for any good defense, today's game is all about speed. Even at the youth level, offenses are getting creative with the way they attack opposing defenses on the edge. The best way to counter that attack is to have fast players on the edges of your defense. Defensive ends are what football savants call "big speed." Ideally, they should look like defensive linemen—tall and broad shouldered—but run like linebackers. Defensive ends should be some of the most versatile players on your defense and often double as tight ends on offense. They have even become particularly hot commodities in the NFL. The Houston Texans used the top overall pick in the 2006 NFL Draft to select Mario Williams, an end out of North Carolina State, over Heisman Trophy winner Reggie Bush.

In an ideal setting, defensive ends should be able to play the run, rush the passer, and drop back into coverage when needed. It's a lot to ask of a young player, so start simple with your ends and expand their roles as they become more comfortable with each aspect of playing the position.

Linebackers

As mentioned earlier in this chapter, defensive linemen are the building blocks of a dominant unit, but linebackers are the heart and soul of any shutdown defense. They make the big plays, and most defenses are designed to funnel the ballcarrier in the direction of the linebackers so they can clean up the play. Linebackers will typically lead your team in tackles and may be asked to do a variety of tasks, including blitzing and covering the tight end on passing plays. For that very reason, linebackers are generally the most well-rounded athletes on a defense. They don't need the same kind of height that defensive linemen have, but they need strength, speed, and intelligence to play the position effectively.

Most teams run defenses that employ either three or four linebackers who line up behind the defensive line and in front of the defensive backfield, about 5 or 6 yards off the ball. A linebacker must utilize the proper ready position as shown in figure 4.9 in order to react quickly to what is developing in front of him. He should have his knees bent, back straight,

Figure 4.9 Proper ready position for a linebacker.

and head forward. Arms should be out in front, and his weight should be on the balls of the feet so he is ready to explode in any direction.

Linebackers must be able to move quickly, both vertically and laterally. This requires good burst and even better hip movement. Much like running back, linebacker is a position that requires players to change direction rapidly and without thinking. A linebacker should be able to turn his body and run side to side without taking his eyes off the football (see figure 4.10). Linebackers should constantly be reading the offense, looking for hints as to what the play might be. After the snap, they should be quick with play recognition and have the ability to locate the ball at all times.

Today's offenses are designed to fool the defense. Fake handoffs, side steps, and reverses are all meant to keep the defense off balance, which is why the linebackers must be able to see these tricks coming ahead of time so that they, and the rest of the defense, have time to react. It's unrealistic to expect your young linebackers to have those natural instincts at this stage, but a coach can help foster the early stages of play recognition by teaching his players to look for the right keys. Quarterbacks are taught to carry out their ball fakes because too many defensive players

Figure 4.10   A linebacker should keep his eyes on the ball while moving sideways.

are like fans: They lock their eyes onto the quarterback and lose sight of what is happening around him.

Defensive Backs

The defensive backs, also known as the secondary, are the last line of defense. Their job is to make sure no one from the offense gets between them and the end zone, which is an important job when the first priority is to keep teams out of the end zone. The secondary consists of two groups of defensive backs. The ones at the back of the formation are safeties and the ones playing closer to the line of scrimmage are cornerbacks. Both groups are essential for good pass defense, although it's unlikely at the youth football level that your team will encounter many high-impact passing attacks.

Cornerbacks

Now that you have established a solid front seven, it's time to work on the back end of your defense. Considering today's rules about contact and coverage, it would be hard to say generally that defensive backs are as important as linebackers or defensive linemen, but try running an effective defense without good cornerbacks and you'll quickly find out how imperative they can be. A cornerback's primary job is to keep the receiver across from him from catching the ball. That task is altered slightly when operating out of a zone defense, as opposed to a man defense, but by and large the goal of every cornerback is to keep the ball from being caught downfield.

In man-to-man (or single) coverage, a cornerback is responsible for shadowing the specific wide receiver to which he is assigned. When working with kids in this age group, you won't want to complicate things too much, so have them physically point to the player across from them, and let them know they should follow that player wherever he goes. It might seem a little simplistic for football, but kids understand the concept of being responsible for one other person much better than they do being part of the overall scheme on defense. If you choose to be a brave soul and incorporate a zone look to your defense, corners would then be assigned to an area of the field rather than a specific player. Their job would be to protect that area and prevent any player who enters it from catching the ball.

The stance for a cornerback is quite similar to that of a linebacker, except that the player stands more upright as shown in figure 4.11. Knees are still slightly bent, chest is out, head is up, and hands are in

Figure 4.11 Correct stance for a cornerback.

front ready to go to work against a receiver (within the first 5 yards). Corners must learn to run on the balls of their feet, and they must develop fluid hip movements if they want to keep pace with bigger, sometimes quicker wide receivers.

Corners must also perfect the art of backpedaling like no other player on the football field. This skill should be practiced daily, as should changing direction. Cornerback can be one of the most challenging positions for young players to learn because they don't fully understand how to control certain parts of their bodies. Backpedaling and changing direction at the same time will be a tough task for many kids.

Take extra time to help them learn the proper footwork and to make sure they know that a cornerback should never turn his back to the quarterback. Instead, he should turn his hips perpendicular to the direction of the movement while keeping his head focused in the direction of the quarterback. Bodyweight should be equally distributed on both feet. When coming out of a backpedal, players should plant on the ball of their back foot (never on the heel) and explode forward off the back foot.

Safeties

A safety is a bit of a cross between a linebacker and a cornerback. Safeties line up 10 to 12 yards from the line of scrimmage—directly behind the linebackers (see figure 4.12)—and much like cornerbacks, safeties are responsible for defending the pass first and the run second. They are the last line of defense, and their number one challenge is to ensure that nothing gets over their heads, particularly when the defense is aligned in a Cover-2 look, which means both safeties are dropping back to defend against deep routes.

The free safety acts as a centerfielder, responsible for watching the whole field and making a play for any ball within range. Typically, the strong safety is a bit larger and ideally stronger than the free safety, as he is asked to help more against the run, although the term *strong* is used because the player lines up on the strong side of the offense, which is the side where the tight end is lined up (figure 4.12). Almost every defense at every level has at least two cornerbacks and two safeties on the field at all times.

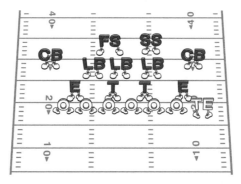

Figure 4.12 The safeties line up 10 to 12 yards behind the line of scrimmage, and the strong safety lines up on the same side of the field as the tight end.

Drill 1 Slalom Course

EQUIPMENT   3-5 cones; footballs (optional)

PURPOSE   Building endurance and agility while teaching kids to work on speed, balance, and technique (this drill allows you to teach footwork, change of direction, and velocity)

PROCEDURE   Set up three to five cones in a zigzag line approximately 5 yards apart down the field. Players line up about 5 yards before the first cone and weave their way through the cones one by one before sprinting back to the starting line as fast as they can. Have the players walk through the slalom course the first time to get a feel for the route. The second time, they should run it while sinking their hips in an athletic stance. The third time through have them do it moving sideways, and the last time through have them try it while backpedaling.

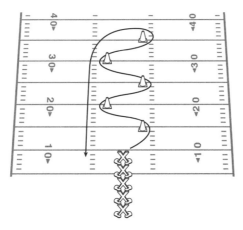

COACHING POINTS   Watch to make sure the players are not running upright when they go through the cones. Look for sharp cuts, and be sure they are opening their hips and keeping their eyes up instead of looking at their feet. On the sideways trip through the cones, be sure the players slide their feet as they move laterally. You may need to do the backpedaling pass several times at first as players get used to changing direction while moving backward.

MODIFICATIONS   To keep the drill interesting, increase or decrease the number of cones. The setup of the cones can change from a straight line to more of an off-road course. You can also practice throwing footballs to the players when they complete the drill (before they sprint back to the line), or have them finish with a tackle.

Drill 2 Come to Balance

EQUIPMENT   None (coach can use a whistle to give commands)

PURPOSE   Teaching defenders to break down and come back to a balanced position before executing a tackle

PROCEDURE   Three or four defenders line up in a straight line across a yard marker facing the coach, who is 15 to 20 yards from the players. The players should start in a good defensive stance, and on the coach's command, they should spring 5 yards forward and then break down and come to balance again by chopping their feet beneath them. On the coach's next command, the players will spring (still using proper technique) all the way past the coach.

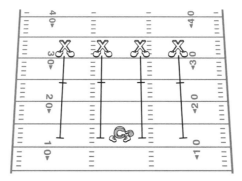

COACHING POINTS   Look for heads to be up at all times. No looking down at the feet. Feet should be shoulder-width apart with knees bent and weight evenly distributed. Players should keep their feet moving throughout the entire drill.

MODIFICATIONS   The drill can be used to help defensive backs work on their backpedal. On the coach's command, have the defensive backs backpedal for 5 yards before coming to balance. Then on the next command, they will backpedal past the coach.

Drill 3 Angle Tackle

EQUIPMENT   1 football; 4 cones

PURPOSE   Teaching defenders how to take good angles and make a proper angle tackle on a ballcarrier

PROCEDURE   Break the team into two equal groups: ballcarriers and defenders. Have the two groups line up, and set up two cones approximately 5 yards apart. Place two more cones halfway between and also 5 yards apart (laterally) so that the four cones form a diamond shape. The first players in each line should step up to the cones and face each other with the coach standing behind the defender. The coach should then signal which direction the ballcarrier should run without the defender's seeing. When the coach gives the signal, the ballcarrier should run diagonally toward the cone in the direction the coach had signaled. The defender should then move in to make the angle tackle. After the tackle, the ballcarrier gives the ball to the next ballcarrier; the first ballcarrier and defender go to the end of the opposite line. Run the drill enough times so that each player has a chance to be a ballcarrier and a defender.

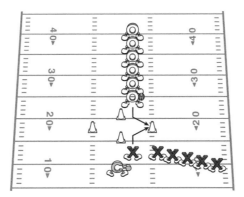

COACHING POINTS   Be sure to watch for proper tackling technique. The defender should stay on the back-side of the ballcarrier with his helmet across the player's body. At no time should the defender ever lower his helmet to make the hit. Watch for the defender to wrap up and drive his legs through the ballcarrier until the tackle is made.

MODIFICATIONS   To make the drill more challenging, change the angle of the ballcarrier's route or the distance the defender must cover to get to the ballcarrier.

Drill 4 Oklahoma

EQUIPMENT   2 blocking bags

PURPOSE   Teaching defenders to get off blocks and deliver a hit; teaching defenders to bring the ballcarrier to the ground

PROCEDURE   Divide your players equally into an offense and defense. This drill is competitive, so divide your players according to whether they're more likely to play offense or defense. From the offensive group, select a blocker, a quarterback, and a running back; from the defensive group, select a defensive lineman and a linebacker. Set up two blocking bags

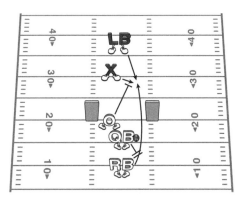

5 yards apart to represent the hole through which the running back must run. The quarterback should start with the ball and hand off to the running back while the offensive lineman blocks. The defensive lineman should attempt to shed the block and make the tackle in the backfield. If he fails, the linebacker must stop the running back from getting past him. Run the drill until all players get a chance to play both positions on offense and defense.

COACHING POINTS   This drill is excellent to introduce kids to the concepts of coming off blocks and making a tackle. Keep score but also look for proper technique. Defenders should stay low and bend their knees. They should wrap up and drive their legs through the ballcarrier. All players involved should keep their heads up and feet moving at all times. You want to keep things physical, but don't let the players go overboard and risk someone getting hurt.

MODIFICATIONS   Add two blockers and an extra defender to make the drill more intense.

Drill 5 Explosive Step

EQUIPMENT   1 football; 1 long piece of string or rope

PURPOSE   Teaching defensive linemen to explode off the ball without going offside

PROCEDURE   Tie the string (or rope) around the ball, and divide your defensive players (which might be all of your players) into groups of three or four. Start the drill with one group by setting the ball down in front of them. They should line up across from it as the defensive line would in a game. After the players are set, pull the string to move the ball away from them. As soon as they see the ball move (and not before), players should explode across the line of scrimmage. After players have the hang of this drill, you can bark out numbers and words to simulate an actual cadence in an attempt to get the defensive linemen to jump offside. If one of the players jumps offside before the ball moves, have the group try again. If all players explode out of their stance on the movement of the ball, they should continue working 2 to 3 yards upfield in their stance. Then, the next group moves in to do the drill.

COACHING POINTS   Watch to make sure the players are using the correct stance when they line up before the snap and when they explode off the ball. Make sure the players respond only to the ball and not to the coach's cadence. They should not cross the line of scrimmage before the ball moves, and they should also be aware of the neutral zone. Make sure the players stay low and drive their legs as they come hard off the ball.

MODIFICATIONS   To work on timing their movement based on an offensive player, pair up your players and have the partners line up across from each other. One partner is the defensive lineman, and the other is the offensive lineman. The players get into a ready position. The coach still calls out the cadence, but the defensive player reacts to the offensive player's movement instead of to the ball.

Drill 6 Tennis Ball Drop

EQUIPMENT   1 tennis ball for every 2 players

PURPOSE   Training kids' bodies to react simultaneously to what they see, especially the movement of a ball

PROCEDURE   Have each player find a partner, and give one tennis ball to each pair. The players should spread out in the designated area, and partners should line up 5 yards apart from each other. One player moves into a three-point stance on an imaginary line of scrimmage, and the partner holds the tennis ball out in front of him at a height above the player's head. When the coach or partner calls out *Hike!* the partner releases the ball, and the other player must explode forward and catch it

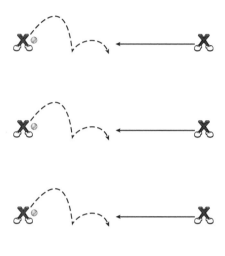

before it bounces twice. It's important that the defender move on movement, not just on the voice of his or her partner. The entire group should do the drill together the first time through, with the coach giving the signal. After that, the partner with the ball can give the command. After each turn, partners switch roles.

COACHING POINTS   Every second counts in football, so watch to make sure the players are getting out of their stance quickly enough to get to the ball. Remember that how long it takes kids to react to what they see is much different from how it is with adults. Just like their eye–hand coordination, their eye–body coordination is still developing. Kids need to practice exploding out of their stance at the very instant their eyes sense movement from the offense.

MODIFICATIONS   For more advanced players, instruct them to catch the ball before it even bounces on the ground once, or have the partner move farther than 5 yards away so they must cover more ground to get the tennis ball.

Drill 7 Man in the Mirror

EQUIPMENT 1 football; 6 blocking bags (optional)

PURPOSE Teaching linebackers to mirror the path of the ballcarrier and react to his forward movement into a hole or gap

PROCEDURE Align six players (or six blocking bags) in a straight line along one of the yard lines. Leave 1 to 2 feet (.3 to .6 m) between each player (or bag) so that it looks like an actual offensive line plus a tight end. Have one player act as the running back by lining up 5 yards deep to one side of the line with the ball in his hands. Linebackers should form a line out of the way. The first linebacker lines up in front of the offensive line on the opposite side of the running back. When the coach says *Hike!* the running back should move behind the line before selecting a gap to run through. The linebacker should mirror the exact path of the ballcarrier, and when the running back steps up into a gap, the linebacker should step up into that hole to meet him.

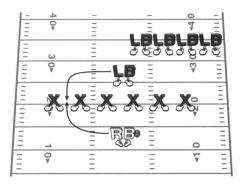

COACHING POINTS The linebacker should keep his eyes glued to the football. Wherever it goes, he goes. Look for a good athletic stance and good footwork. When the running back starts on his path down the line, the linebacker should turn and open his hips to move down the line with him.

MODIFICATIONS Speed up the drill as the players become more comfortable with it. Eventually it is important to run the drill at full speed. You won't want to have full-on collisions in the hole, but adding cuts and possibly tackles to the drill is a good way to practice for the real thing.

Drill 8 The Tip

EQUIPMENT   1 football; 2 cones

PURPOSE   Teaching defenders to break on the ball and catch tipped passes

PROCEDURE   Set up two cones 10 to 15 yards apart, and station a receiver at each cone. Pair up your defensive players, and have the pairs line up off to the side. The first pair takes position one in front of the other about 10 to 15 yards in front of the coach. The partners should have about 5 yards between them, and both partners face the coach. On the coach's command, both players begin backpedaling as if to defend a pass play. The coach, pretending to be the quarterback, turns his body toward one of the receivers and lobs a pass in that direction. The first defender (closest to the coach) closes on the cone and receiver, breaking up the pass by tipping the ball in the air. The second defender comes in behind his partner and intercepts the pass. This pair goes to the back of the line, and the next pair takes a turn.

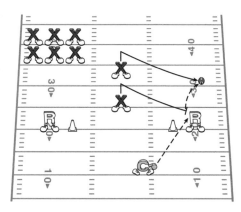

COACHING POINTS   Look for a good backpedal. Eyes should be glued to the quarterback and not looking down at the feet or back over the shoulder. The players must make good breaks once the ball is in the air. "Plant and go" should be the rule. No wasted steps getting out of the backpedal. The defenders should spring to the intended cone. No loafing.

MODIFICATIONS   The drill can also be done with just one defender by having the receiver tip the pass up in the air as if it went off his fingertips. The drill can also be done without the receivers by just having the front defender tip the ball up and over his head to the defender behind him. One other variation is to have the defenders chop their feet in place instead of backpedaling.

Drill 9 The W

EQUIPMENT   1 football; 5 cones

PURPOSE   Teaching defensive backs to break in and out of their backpedal while keeping their eyes focused on the quarterback

PROCEDURE   Set up two cones 5 to 7 yards apart on one of the yard lines. Set three more cones 5 to 7 yards apart and 5 to 7 yards away and staggered from the first set. (The middle cone of the second group should line up with the space in the center of the first set of cones so that all the cones create a W.) Players line up at the first cone on the left. The first player assumes a good defensive stance, facing the players in line behind him. On the coach's command, he backpedals at a 45-degree angle toward the second cone. Then he plants his back foot and sprints on a 45-degree angle to the third cone. The player should break down and come to balance at the third cone before backpedaling to the fourth cone, where he will again plant and sprint to the final cone. He returns to the end of the line, and the next player starts his W course.

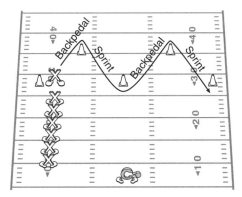

COACHING POINTS   Look for a good stance and backpedal from players. That means butt down, head up, hands out in front, and back straight. Eyes should be forward. If a defensive back must look down at his feet, he will lose track of the ball and the quarterback. Be sure the players plant hard at the first cone and explode into a full sprint as they run to the second cone. Make sure they run all the way through the last cone. No slowing down until they are well beyond the final cone.

MODIFICATIONS   The drill can be done on a smaller scale with only two cones. You can also add a pass or a fumble at the end of the drill so the defender has to sprint through the last cone and either make a catch or scoop up a fumble to complete the drill.

Drill 10 Zigzag

EQUIPMENT   1 football

PURPOSE   Teaching defensive backs to read and react to the quarterback's shoulders while also developing their ability to rotate hips and change direction

PROCEDURE   Form a line of players. The first four players line up along a yard line 5 yards from the coach and with 5 yards between each player. The coach, who is in front of the players and facing them, should hold a ball and pretend to be a quarterback. On the coach's command, the four players (using the proper defensive stance) begin backpedaling, keeping their eyes on the quarterback and the ball. The coach turns his shoulders and the ball to the right or to the left, and the defenders react by opening their hips and backpedaling at a 45-degree angle to the same side as the coach's movement. Then, the coach changes the direction of his shoulders. The defenders must adjust by swinging their hips in the opposite direction to change directions midbackpedal. At the end of the drill, the coach throws the ball to one of the players, and all four sprint past the coach and to the end of the line. Repeat the drill until all players have been through the line.

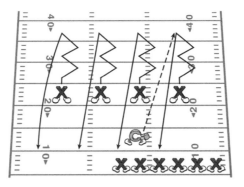

COACHING POINTS   Watch the defenders' eyes to make sure they are reading the quarterback. Make sure the players are not abandoning the proper backpedaling technique because they are thinking too much. Watch to make sure they swivel their hips and open them to the side the quarterback is aiming his shoulders. They must not turn their backs on the quarterback when they change directions.

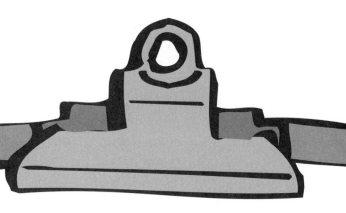

The Coach's Clipboard

✔ The main priority of the defense is to keep the other team out the end zone.

✔ The main priority of the coach is to prevent neck injuries in defensive players.

✔ Defenders should break down at the point of attack by bending their knees, sinking their hips, and arching their backs while keeping their eyes up.

✔ Hits should be made number on number, with the defender's helmet to the side of the ball.

✔ The helmet should never be used as a weapon.

✔ Tacklers should wrap their arms around the ballcarrier's arms at the point of contact while lifting from the ground up.

✔ In a three-point stance, one hand should be on the ground just inside the player's foot and just in front of the player's shoulders. Butt down, back straight, and chest out.

Your Offensive Playbook

Game day is drawing ever closer. Will your kids be ready? This is a recurring question in the minds of many coaches. Even if you have done everything you can to teach your players the fundamentals of playing offense, that doesn't automatically mean they are ready to start moving the ball up and down the field at will. Learning the proper mechanics for throwing a football is a great first step for young quarterbacks, but you can't turn them into a Joe Montana overnight. The same goes for blocking, running the football, and catching passes. These are essential skills that all football players should have, but there is more to running a thriving offense than having a group of players who know the football fundamentals (although it is much, much easier to build up from that than it is to go back and try to teach this stuff later).

To get the ball in the end zone with any consistency, you need to develop an offensive playbook that is both clear-cut and effective. After everything you have been through already as a rookie coach, this may sound like an easy task by comparison, but it can be a complicated one if you don't know where to start. That's what we're here for. Before you get out the chalk, pen, or stick and start drawing up plays like a mad scientist, it's important to remember who will be running these plays. You might feel confident your triple-reverse pass is a thing of wonder, but it doesn't do you any good if your kids can't run it effectively. Assuming you are coaching in a community that values football, or at least has a football program at the high school level, we recommend scheduling a sit-down with the head varsity football coach. This thought may have even crossed your mind, but it was likely dismissed under the pretense of *He's the head varsity football coach; I'm a lowly Pee Wee coach. What interest could he have in taking time out of his busy schedule to talk with me?*

To get past this line of thinking, you need to understand two things. First of all, most coaches love to have their brains picked, especially by other coaches. By nature, the profession lends itself to sharing and copycatting. Second, in the history of football, there have been maybe 10 original ideas; everything else has been morphing and adjusting and building off what other coaches have done. It's the second reason that should make this meeting a must for any high school football coach. It's in the program's best interest to have kids at the Pee Wee and middle school levels learning the same type of offense they will be asked to run at the high school level. Ask the varsity coaching staff for some basic plays they would like to see your team run, and try to base your offensive scheme on what they are doing at the varsity level. It's a win–win situation because it will help you greatly when trying to decide what type of offense to run, and it will help your players if they plan to go on and play football in the community at the middle school, junior varsity, or varsity levels.

Even if you think you have a creative mind when it comes to football offenses, we still recommend trying to incorporate some of what's being done at the high school level, but feel free to make your own adjustments as you get more comfortable in your role as a football coach. If they are running a shotgun offense at the varsity level, but you think a more traditional look will fit your team better, then go with your gut. No one knows your team better than you, and most offenses have the same basic plays anyway; it just depends on the look and formation.

Running Game

If you do decide to utilize the playbook from your local high school program—which we strongly recommend—then you will want to stick with the same terminology they are using at the higher levels as well. This will allow you to gain a full understanding of how plays are called, and it will be an even greater help to your players as they advance in the program. Your goal should be to keep things as simple as possible without skimping on the important stuff. Offensive linemen should have splits of 1 to 2 feet (.3 to .6 m), and those spaces are called gaps. Every running play should have a name followed by a number corresponding to the appropriate gap. The gaps (A, B, and C) can be numbered from the inside out. Plays going to the right use even numbers, and plays going to the left use odd numbers, starting with the two gaps directly beside the center (the A gaps).

The A gap to the left side of the center (odd) becomes gap number 1, with the A gap to the right side of the center (even) labeled number 2 (see figure 5.1). The next step out is the B gap, which marks the opening between the guards and tackles. The B gap to the left (odd) becomes number 3, and the B

Figure 5.1 Numbering for the gaps to the left and right of center.

gap to the right (even) is number 4. If you're scoring at home, the next two gaps would be the C gaps, and of course, the C gap to the left becomes number 5, and the C gap to the right is number 6. These gaps come between the tackles and the tight end or simply just the space outside the tackle if there is no tight end to his side. Thus, the gaps continue from the inside out, going 2, 4, 6, and 8 on the right side of the center and 1, 3, 5, 7 on the left side of the center. Gaps 7 and 8 are used for sweeps or tosses to the outside.

These numbers might seem to make things more complicated initially, but eventually they will make everything much simpler and more concise because they allow you to call plays to a specific side and specific gap without having to spend five minutes explaining the play. When calling the plays, run plays going to the 2 gap (the A gap to the right of the center) end with 2. So, a dive play to the 2 hole (or 2 gap) is a Dive-2 play. A trap to the 1 gap is a Trap-1 play, and so on. Using the gap numbers in the name helps kids who have a hard time remembering the meaning of plays with word names only.

Quick-Hitter

It's important at this level not to spread yourself too thin offensively. NFL playbooks can be dozens of pages thick, if not hundreds, but yours better not fill up much more than the front and back of a page if you want your kids to have any chance of remembering what they should be doing on the field. You will need a go-to play you can fall back on when things get tough, and the first thing every running game must have at any level is a quick-hitting play, or dive play. We recommend using the midline option play (see figure 5.2), but regardless of what play you choose, the basic idea is a quick, hard-hitting play that goes between the guard and tackle split (or B gap).

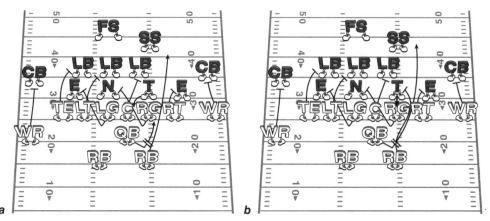

Figure 5.2 In the midline option play, (*a*) if the defensive tackle rushes hard up the middle, the quarterback hands off to the running back or (*b*) if the defensive tackle plays the run, the quarterback fakes the handoff and runs the ball himself.

You should be rotating players through different positions, so it may not always be possible, but the midline option play works best with your top ballcarrier playing quarterback and your second-best ballcarrier lined up behind him at running back. The play itself hinges on what the opposing team's best 3-technique defensive tackle does. It might sound strange, but your offensive line will not actually attempt to block this player at the point of attack. Instead, it is the quarterback's job to read him, making him the key for the offense. If the defensive tackle is rushing hard up the middle at the quarterback, the running back should have a big day taking the handoff and running the football right past him. If the tackle is playing the run, and therefore keying the running back, your quarterback will fake the handoff, after which he should be able to step up and slip past the defensive tackle at the line of scrimmage using the running back as a lead blocker.

Keep in mind that the success of this play is largely predicated on finding a quarterback who can read the play and decide whether to keep the ball or hand it off. From where you're standing, that might seem like a tough task for kids at this age, but it will be a lot easier to find a player who can make that read than to find a kid who can sprint out and throw a strong, accurate pass on the run. Although the play is designed as a sure-bet quick-hitter, it also provides the kind of unpredictability needed to survive in today's football world, as the defense can't predetermine on any given play whether the quarterback is going to keep the ball or hand it off to the running back. Ultimately, the idea is to force the defensive tackle to choose between tackling the dive back or the quarterback. Whomever he leaves alone should have a nice hole to run through.

One issue you are likely to encounter with this play is a running back who wants to take the handoff every time instead of leaving the decision up to the quarterback. Most young players don't understand the idea of a fake handoff, so explain to them that the dive back should not take the football from the quarterback but rather wait for the quarterback to give it to him. Your players will need to practice this play frequently if it is going to be one of your go-to plays. This is also a fine opportunity to introduce your team, especially your quarterbacks, to the concept of reading keys, something that will also translate to the passing game.

Trap Play

The second thing every offense should have at this level is a trap play, and it very well could turn out to be the best play in your entire playbook. If you are going to run a quick-hitting play right at the belly of the opposing defense, then you definitely should have a trap play that looks just like it. Once you have run your quick-hitting play enough that the defense is starting to key on it—there's that word again—you have the defense set up perfectly for a trap play. This is a play designed to look identical to your quick-hitting play except that the ball will actually go the opposite way of where you have been running, as shown in figure 5.3.

Trap plays are especially successful if the defense cannot distinguish that a new play is being run, but in order to fool them, everything must look the same. This is where the reverse step or cut from chapter 3 comes into play. The running back should take a hard jab-step in the direction of the original midline option play before reversing field to the opposite side. A jab-step involves a running back's planting hard with his lead foot as if the running play is going one direction before cutting back in the direction of the actual play (i.e., if the trap play is really designed to go to the left, the back should jab-step hard with his right foot as if the play were called to the right).

The trap is an excellent play at the youth football level for a variety of reasons. It is simple to teach and nearly impossible to defend. That's right, *impossible*. If you run it correctly, alongside the midline option play, there is no reason your running back can't average 10 yards per carry

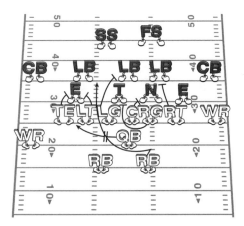

Figure 5.3 The trap play is run to the opposite side as your quick-hitting play.

on trap plays. What's that? Your offensive line isn't very good? Well, fortunately, pulling (when a lineman moves back and over to block an area other than his usual position) is a very easy thing to teach young offensive linemen. Once you find a kid who can do it well, you can trap the heck out of your opponents.

What if the opposing players are bigger, faster, and stronger than your team? Unlike in most other plays, this can actually work to your advantage with the trap play. If you are facing a monster defensive tackle who seems to be in your backfield on every play, hit him with a couple of trap plays, and all of a sudden he won't be as aggressive anymore (getting blindsided by a pulling guard tends to have that effect). Once he starts trying to read the play to see if a pulling guard is coming his way, blast him with a double-team block and drive him 5 yards off the ball. That should have his head swimming enough that your offense can get back to business. When your offense is struggling, you may find yourself trapping on nearly half of the plays because it seems to be the only thing working.

Off-Tackle Play

Relying on the midline option and trap plays to carry your running game is a good start, but what happens when the defense decides to spy (mirroring his every move) your quarterback with its best athlete while simultaneously blitzing both A gaps? The end result could be disastrous for your offense. Most likely you are looking at a loss of yards or even a turnover. The best way to counter this, or better yet prevent it from happening, is to beat the defense on the outside or, at the very least, force them to defend the edge. An off-tackle-play (see figure 5.4) is a little bit wider than the midline option or trap play but not quite as wide as a sweep or toss play. These are often the plays no one likes when they see them on TV, but they can be very effective at the youth football level.

The off-tackle play attacks the defense through one of the two C gaps located just to the outside of the offensive tackles (hence the name *off-tackle*). An off-tackle play to the left is designed for the running back to hit the 5 gap—remember, odd numbers to the left, even numbers to the right—through a hole created by the offensive tackle and tight end, while an

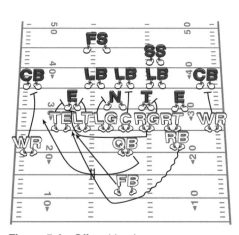

Figure 5.4   Off-tackle play.

off-tackle play to the right would go to the 6 hole. Unlike a sweep or toss play, the off-tackle play requires specific blocks on the outside in order to create the hole for the running back to run through. In most playbooks, the off-tackle play includes a double-team block by the offensive tackle and tight end at the point of attack (one of the two C gaps) followed by a kick-out block on the outside linebacker by the lead blocker (typically the fullback). The back-side guard should pull to the play side and follow the fullback through the hole in order to spring the running back free once he clears the line of scrimmage.

In a standard offense—whether that be the split-back, I-formation, or wishbone—where the quarterback is under center, the veer option can be used as a form of off-tackle. Also known as the triple option, the veer was invented by University of Houston coach Bill Yeoman in 1964 and is often referred to as the Houston veer. It introduced the football world to the idea of having the quarterback read one or two players on the defense before deciding what to do with the football. It was made famous by coach Jack Lengyel in 1971 when he implemented Bobby Bowden's system at Marshall after the devastating plane crash that killed most of the school's coaches and players. Lengyel switched from the I-formation to the veer because he thought it would help even the playing field for his group of undersized, and ultimately less talented, replacement players. This works because the veer relies on precision and execution rather than pure athleticism by using combination blocks and double teams up front. It is similar to the midline option play in that one back takes the dive course and the quarterback will read the defense before deciding where the football should go. Unlike the midline option, however, the veer option gives the quarterback more choices because there are three running backs on the play (see figure 5.5). Along with the dive back, there

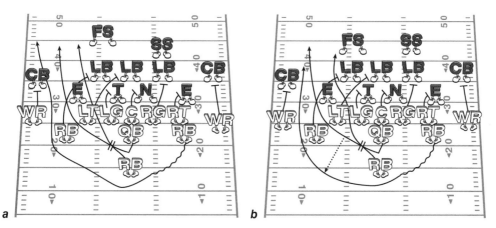

Figure 5.5 For the veer option, (*a*) the quarterback can make a handoff to the dive back, fake the handoff, and run the ball himself, or (*b*) fake the handoff to the dive back and then pitch to the outside.

will be another option to pitch the ball to the outside, with the third back turning into a lead blocker for the ballcarrier on the perimeter.

This play can also be run out of the spread offense as a dart play, or zone read, similar to what Vince Young ran at Texas or Juice Williams at Illinois. The zone read, which has become exceedingly popular under the name Wildcat, is actually a rather simplistic football play along the lines of the midline option. The quarterback takes the snap and reads what the weak-side defensive end (see figure 5.6) is doing (*weak side* meaning side with fewer players). If the end attacks, the quarterback keeps the ball and runs it himself. If the end plays contain, the quarterback hands it off to the tailback. Like the veer, this can be a great way to attack quick defenses that tend to overpursue because it punishes defenders for being out of position or for chasing the ball. Just know that there are risks involved in using an offense like this with kids in this age group. If you're going to be pitching and faking the ball all over the place, it is inevitably going to find its way to the ground, so don't forget the

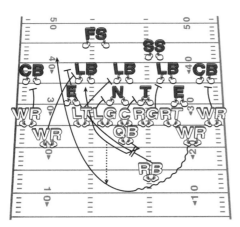

Figure 5.6   The veer option from the spread offense has the same option as the original veer: The quarterback can use a handoff, run the ball himself, or make a pitch to the outside.

antacid pills at home. If you can't handle the idea of a few more turnovers—and some coaches really cannot—then the veer and zone-read plays are probably not for you. In that case, you'll want to stick to the more traditional handoffs.

Sweep Plays

A traditional sweep or toss play (also known as student body right or student body left) is exactly what it sounds like. The play is designed to attack the edge of the defense, so the quarterback takes a few steps down the line and pitches the ball to the running back, who is running parallel to the line of scrimmage. This play is typically run out of the single-back, split-back, or I-formation and works best when you have a running back with some speed. That might sound like a no-brainer, since it always helps to have a running back with speed, but the pitch play can utilize a fast player on your team who might not have the best vision or ability to break tackles. With the new focus being on misdirection, traditional sweep and toss plays (which focus on speed) have become less common at the professional and college levels, but they are still wonderfully valuable in youth football. At this level of football, having one extremely fast kid who can get to the edge and turn right or left might be all you need to put four or five touchdowns on the board.

If your quarterback can perfect the art of pitching the ball—which definitely takes some practice—and your speedster can consistently catch the pitch and tuck the ball away, you could be looking at the golden ticket. Making a good pitch requires a certain amount of balance. The quarterback should be waiting until the end commits to tackling him before he pitches to the tailback (or else the end can just run after the tailback), which means he could be getting hit already by the time he lets go of the ball. The pitch should be thrown with the outside arm and the quarterback should shield his body as he flips the ball (see figure 5.7). It's important that he aim for the player's numbers, or chest. If he throws it too high or too low, you could be looking at a turnover, so accuracy is critical.

No matter how much time coaches spend coaching defense and teaching their players about spacing and angles and pursuit, kids at this level are still going to see that ball and run right at it. With this in mind, a player who can take a pitch and outrun everyone to the sideline will be a terrifically dangerous weapon for your offense. By the time he gets to the edge and turns upfield, there should be nothing but daylight in front of him, especially if your blockers are doing their jobs.

It's unlikely your team will be using any zone blocking on the offensive line, so the sweep play will call for at least one of the guards to pull with the

Figure 5.7   Quarterback pitching the ball to the tailback.

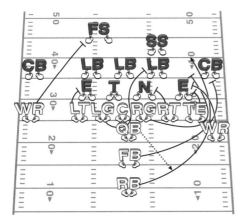

Figure 5.8 Sweep play.

other linemen blocking down on their man. If you choose to pull both guards—which is recommended on most sweeps—the back-side guard should pick up the play-side linebacker so that the play-side guard can get outside and lead the way down the sideline (see figure 5.8). The fullback would eventually follow the play-side guard to the outside, but his primary responsibility on the play is to ensure that your running back actually makes it to the outside without being tackled, and he does this by picking up any defenders who have penetrated the backfield. The faster your running back, the less precise your blockers will need to be. If you've got the next Reggie Bush in your backfield, there are times where you can just give him the ball and get out of his way. Unlike a handoff, a pitch will allow him to get the ball in motion and then run to the sideline and turn upfield before the defense knows what hit them.

Counter Play

Unlike the sweep play, a counter play relies entirely on precision and 11 players doing their jobs in order to be successful. A quick counter typically involves a running back in the backfield who will serve as the decoy and another in the slot position who will get the football (see figure 5.9). It can also include wide receivers and flankers in the same way Florida used Percy Harvin during its run to the 2008 NCAA National Championship. The quarterback will fake the handoff on one side to the running back coming out of the backfield, and it's important for the running back to sell the fake by hitting the hole hard (the hole is typically an A gap between the center and one of the two guards). The quarterback keeps the ball and gives it to the slot back (or wide receiver) heading in the other direction.

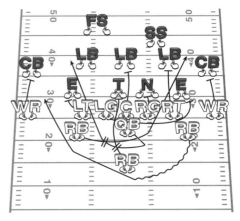

Figure 5.9 Counter play.

The purpose of the play is to get the defense shifting one direction with a ball fake before going back the other way. The quarterback should turn his back to the defense so they have a hard time picking up where the ball is going. Up front, the play-side offensive tackle must pick up the linebacker, but the key to the play is the pulling guard from the back side. It's imperative that he come down the line and blast the defensive end in the 5 hole, or else the entire play could fall apart. Like the trap play, the counter should work well against defenses that like to overpursue, but unlike the trap, it probably will not be an effective play for your offense when facing better teams. If the defense does not buy the ball fake or if one player misses his block up front, the whole thing could come crashing down.

Unlike the trap play, which you may find yourself using as much as 40 to 50 percent of the time in tight situations, the counter works best in a limited capacity. Too much of the play's success depends on execution for you to expect your team to be capable of running a counter 20 times a game, but there's no reason you can't get away with running it 3 or 4 times a game with considerable success if you're willing to put in the time in practice.

Passing Game

In the world of youth football, it's much more important to have a dynamic running game than a potent passing attack. That might sound like an audacious statement, but it's true. Even if you're lucky enough to find a kid on your roster with a rocket arm, the chances are slim to none that he will be the same kid who can call the plays, read the defense, run the football, and manage the game, not to mention make accurate throws in the short to intermediate passing game. If you have your best player at quarterback, your offense will probably end up looking more like West Virginia's under Pat White than the Colts' under Peyton Manning. Obviously it's never going to operate as smoothly or fruitfully as a collegiate or NFL offense, but the idea is that very few youth football teams can throw the ball 40 times and be effective. Finding an athlete who can run the offense and make a few key throws is essential.

Short Game

Watching teams "air it out" on TV might be fun when you're sitting on your couch at home. Watching your youth football team try it from the sideline on game day will be anything but. The best passing play at this level of the game is the 3-yard stop, as shown in figure 5.10. It might sound old-

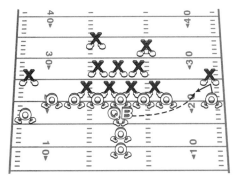

Figure 5.10 The 3-yard stop.

fashioned, and maybe it is, but we believe it is the building block for all passing games. Forget the long touchdown passes you see on Sundays; if your team can run this play successfully, you will be on your way to having a dangerous balance on offense. The 3-yard stop might not seem like a real game changer, but it certainly can be if used correctly.

It is an easy way for your young wide outs to get open, and it's a simple pass for your quarterback to complete because it's not a long throw.

The key for the wide receiver is to make the defense think your team is going deep by bursting off the line in the direction of the nearest defensive back. After 3 yards, the receiver stops on a dime and turns back for the football (much like a hook or curl route, except shorter). The play is already about as safe as a passing play can be; however, to further avoid the risk of throwing an interception, the quarterback should aim to throw the ball low and inside so that his receiver is the only one who can catch it. You could literally run this play on every down with at least a 50 percent conversion rate, but most coaches don't have the patience to stick with it. We don't recommend running it every play, but if you've got a good quarterback and even average receivers, this is almost an unstoppable play.

The same type of thinking applies for out routes (see figure 5.11). Receivers should burst off the line as if they are going deep, only to break off their routes after 3 to 4 yards and turn toward the nearest sideline. The receiver should plant on his inside foot to break to the outside. Like the stop route, this is one of the safest routes in all of football and a coach's favorite for that very reason. The quarterback should aim to throw the ball high and to the outside so that either his receiver catches it or the ball sails harmlessly out of bounds. The difference between the out route and the 3-yard stop is the throw. The stop play is one of the easiest throws there is in football, but the out route can be one of the most difficult throws, especially for young quarterbacks. It is a strange angle that often requires quarterbacks to

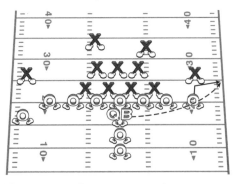

Figure 5.11 Out route pass play.

throw across their bodies, and it calls for a pass that is hard but not too hard. It's a good play to have in the arsenal, but understand that it does not come with a high success rate with kids this young.

Going Deep

The short passing game can not only be an effective tool for moving the ball down the field but can also help you set up your intermediate and deep passes, should you need them. Of course, at this level, the deep passing game won't consist of the 60-yard bombs you see on Sundays. Although Manning and Tom Brady can sling the ball 50 yards down the field with the flick of a wrist, your quarterbacks will struggle to get it 20 yards, so even deep routes should get cut off around 15 to 20 yards. The defense has to respect the offense's ability and willingness to throw the ball short or they will drop their defensive backs so far off your receivers that you will never get a pass over their heads. If you execute your short passing game with any success, sit back and watch with joy as the opposing team moves its safeties closer and closer to the line of scrimmage. Smile with the knowledge that when the time is right, you will hit them for a big one over the top of the defense.

If you've got a kid who can flat-out run—maybe it's the same kid you used for the sweep play—and a quarterback who can get the ball downfield, then keep the go route in mind. This route is also called a fade or streak, and it looks just like it sounds. As shown in figure 5.12, a player takes off in a straight line down the sideline, and the quarterback heaves the ball as far as he can in the receiver's general direction (that's about as much as you can hope for with kids). If everything lines up, the safeties will be out of position and your speedy wide out will run under the ball and take off for the touchdown. It's anything but a guarantee, but if you've got a quicker way to put 6 points on the board, please let us know.

From the moment you introduce them to it, most of the kids on your team will want to run the go route on every snap during practice if you'll let them, but not every kid on your team is built to run it in a game. That doesn't mean smaller or slower players can't contribute in the deep or intermediate passing game. Double moves are a great way for kids with limited ability to get open, and these plays simply aren't utilized enough, even at the high

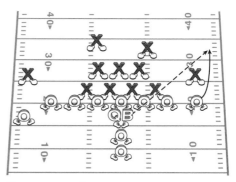

Figure 5.12   Go route pass play.

school level, let alone the youth level. Spend time working with your receivers on how to use a fake to get open. Routes such as the stop-and-go, in-and-out, out-and-up, hitch-and-go, post-flag, and slant-and-go are all routes that work in backyard football, but many coaches tend not to use them because they consider them too elementary. Don't fall victim to this thinking, Coach—be open to thinking outside the box. Double moves have a place in football, especially at the youth level.

Reading the Defense

Earlier in the chapter, we talked about the notion of asking your quarterback to read the defensive tackle on the midline option play before deciding where the ball should go. That concept will prove valuable for your passing game as well. One of the toughest things about playing quarterback is learning to read the defense. Even quarterbacks at the college level still struggle with this aspect of playing the position. It's much easier for a quarterback to figure out what he is doing and where the ball should go when he has an idea of what the defense is trying to do.

At the higher levels, reading the defense becomes more difficult because defensive coordinators will attempt to disguise what they are doing. You're unlikely to see too much of that at the youth football level, so now is a good time to introduce the concept to your young signal callers. Start with something simple, and build from there. If they understand the concept of the midline option, give them a similar teaching point in the passing game. If the defensive back stays tight, the wide receiver should go deep. If the corner backpedals off the line, the wide out should run a stop route. That might seem like something that's more for the receiver to understand, but a big part of becoming a quarterback is understanding where the other 10 players on offense are going to be.

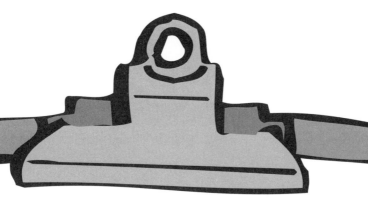

The Coach's Clipboard

✔ Sit down with the varsity football coach in your community to see what offense he is running at the high school level.

✔ Offensive linemen should have splits of 1 to 2 feet (.3 to .6 m) between them.

✔ The gaps (A, B, and C) can be numbered from the inside out.

✔ Plays going to the right use even numbers, and plays going to the left use odd numbers, starting with the two gaps directly beside the center (the A gaps).

✔ When things get tough, you need a go-to play that is a quick, hard-hitting play that goes between the guard and tackle split.

✔ Every offense needs a trap play that is designed to look like your quick-hitting play but goes to the opposite side.

✔ The best passing play at this level is the 3-yard stop.

✔ An effective running game or short passing game can help set up the deep passing game.

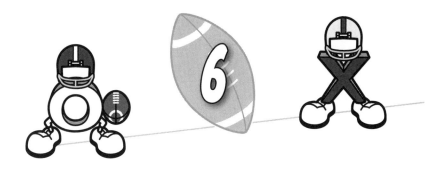

Surefire Defensive Alignments

The previous chapter outlines a surefire offensive playbook to help get your players, and the ball, into the end zone. But as you should know by now, defense wins championships. Even with the right coaching, execution on offense is going to be a struggle, especially early in the season. Just when you think you've got that perfect play called against the ideal defensive look, your best player will drop the ball on the ground for no apparent reason. That's just part of learning to play the game, so it's important to have a strong defense to fall back on. Teaching your players the fundamentals of tackling and getting off blocks is the foundation for that defense, but you're going to need a game plan if you want to avoid having things break down on game days.

Base Defense

Not unlike your players, successful defenses come in all shapes and sizes. Over the years, they have morphed in an attempt to keep up with, or in a few cases get ahead of, offensive innovations. Some coordinators rely on multiple defensive sets in an attempt to confuse the opposing offense, while others stick with one or two looks that work best for them. Traditional minds gravitate toward the 4-3 defense (four down linemen and three linebackers; see figure 6.1), but look no further than the 3-4 defense (three down linemen and four linebackers; see figure 6.2) for the latest NFL trend. There are no fewer than a dozen different defenses being played across the college football landscape at any given time, but even the most complex schemes must have a base set from which they build.

Once again, we recommend checking with the varsity coaching staff in your community before deciding which defense to employ. It may not be as imperative to synchronize things on defense as it is on offense, but it definitely can't hurt for kids to start learning the terminology they will use at the higher levels. Most linebacker breakdowns are pretty standard: middle linebackers are called Mikes, strong-side linebackers become Sams, and weak-side linebackers are Wills, but other positions such as Rovers, Stars, and Vipers are very team specific. The strong side of the field simply refers to the side with more offensive players, while the weak side refers to the side wither fewer offensive players.

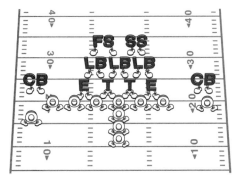

Figure 6.1   Setup for the 4-3 defense.

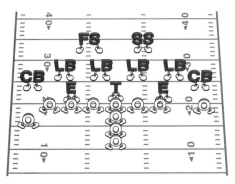

Figure 6.2   Setup for the 3-4 defense.

Very few high school programs run a 3-4 defense because it puts a premium on having speed and athleticism at the linebacker position along with a dominant nose tackle. The 4-3 set, or even the 5-2 (see figure 6.3), is a much more popular option at the high school level because it allows the defensive line to control the tempo of the game.

At this level, we do not recommend teaching kids to blitz unless it is a staple of the high school program. It might sound outdated in today's "get to the quarterback or perish" mentality, but blitzing with kids this age will make your defense very susceptible to big plays. You may

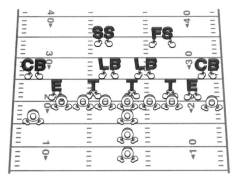

Figure 6.3   Setup for the 5-2 defense.

decide to have a few blitzes in your defensive package (it's always good to be ready for everything) to give your kids something else to get excited about; we're not talking about world-class athletes here. Sacking the quarterback is sure to give your defense an emotional boost, but blitzes are not all that difficult to stop at this level (especially because they are very hard to disguise). If the opposing coach is worth his clipboard, he will simply instruct his offensive linemen to block down. We believe it's more important for you to find out how good your defense is at executing your concept, so spend more time teaching them how to read keys and fill gaps than how to blitz.

Defensive Front

It should not come as a surprise that if your team is going to run an effective 4-3 defense, it must start up front on the defensive line. Although NFL defensive fronts often consist of multiple 300-pounders, there is more to playing up front than being big. You might find that when you put your biggest guy in the trenches, he routinely gets pushed back by smaller, weaker offensive linemen. Don't write him off, because he could learn to become a very good defensive lineman with the right teaching. However, there may be smaller players on your team who are better equipped to handle the position.

What does being better equipped to handle the position mean? Most good defensive coaches will tell you that playing defensive line takes a different mentality than playing offensive line, much like playing defense, in general, is usually reserved for players with a different mind-set than the players on the other side of the ball. It takes toughness, it takes tenacity, and it takes heart. Playing in the trenches is about leverage, technique, playing low, and playing with determination. When you've been around football long enough, you're sure to hear phrases such as "low man wins" and this guy has "an engine that never quits." Nowhere on the football field are these things more important than on the defensive line, where the primary goal is disruption. Does it help to have a big guy who can take up space and eat up blockers on the defensive front? Absolutely, but if you can find smaller guys who can disrupt what the offensive line wants to do, they can be just as effective.

Defensive Tackle   In a 4-3 defense, there are two types of defensive tackles on your front line. These players generally play inside of the two defensive ends, and their primary jobs are to close holes in the running game, keep blockers off your linebackers, and occasionally pressure the quarterback up the middle. If great defenses are built from the inside out, this would truly be your starting point.

The first type of defensive tackle you are looking for is a nose man, or nose tackle. Ideally, this is that big, strong beast of a player who can take on two blockers at the same time. In the NFL, this would be your 350-pound monster such as Shaun Rogers, Albert Haynesworth, or Casey Hampton, but throughout history the position has been played by smaller players such as "Mean" Joe Greene and Randy White. This player must have good balance and great technique, since he should be an immovable object. It doesn't have to be a really athletic kid or even a really talented kid; in fact you might want to save those kids for other positions where their athleticism can be put to better use, because a nose tackle is generally a 1-gap player. Being strong would help, but the position can be filled by a quick kid or a little kid who plays low, uses good technique, and plays with heart and determination. At this level, more often than not, those things will win out over being big and strong. A good nose tackle will play with his eyes up, reading the backfield, even while engaged in a block. Teach him to use his hands to shed blocks and to get his hands up in the pass lanes when a quarterback is winding back for his throw. If you cannot get pressure up the middle with your tackles, a good quarterback will be able to step up in the pocket, and your defensive ends will fly right by him. With a nice push up the middle from the tackles, opposing quarterbacks should be in prime position for your rush ends coming off the edge.

The other defensive tackle spot is similar but slightly different. This will be a 3-technique guy with one hand in the dirt, and this should be one of your studs (assuming you have studs, which not every coach is fortunate enough to say). This is another player who cannot be afraid to take on two blockers, but unlike the nose tackle, this player needs to do more than just occupy that space. He needs to be able to beat those blockers and make a play, whether it be on the running back or the quarterback. Speed is definitely a nice asset for this type of player to have, but he must play with discipline, or good opposing coaches will use his speed against him by running a trap play to his gap. (Of course, as we note in the previous chapter, you'll get to do the same when you're facing a dominant defensive tackle.)

Defensive End   Long overlooked, the defensive end position has gained exposure over the last 20 years because of the emphasis on the sack, but defensive ends are about so much more than just bringing the quarterback to the ground. Obviously putting pressure on the passer and forcing him to alter his reads is the biggest way these players can influence the game, but you need to have defensive ends who can protect the outside and play against the run as well. Like tackles, there are typically two different types of defensive ends in the 4-3 defense.

The first type of end is a strong-side defensive end. This is typically a bigger player than the other end. He should be capable of rushing the quarterback but also dependable when it comes to protecting the outside, playing contain, and stopping the run. Although he may not be your most talented player up front, he should be the most complete player, with the ability to run down ballcarriers on the outside, rush the passer, and take on the trap block. He might lack the natural instincts of your other end, but he should be an intelligent player who plays with discipline and does not get out of position.

On the opposite side is your weak-side defensive end, or Leo. In many cases, this will be the best player on your entire defense and your most dangerous pass rusher. He should be one of your most instinctive players, with great speed and an intense desire. Obviously, when you're dealing with kids, this will all be relative. You're not going to have a roster full of fast kids, so you have to decide which ones will make good linebackers, which ones will make good defensive backs, and which ones might make a good Leo. If a kid is not very fast but has a good first step, he might be a good fit for the Leo assuming you're short on speed. The Leo is a player who excels at getting around offensive linemen when he has a hand down in a three-point stance, but he can also pick his hand up and play like a blitzing outside linebacker if you decide to change the look defensively. You shouldn't be changing too much schematically on game days or your players will get lost, but if you can get your Leo to understand the two different roles, you won't have to change anything in your overall scheme. Either way, your Leo must be a player who can stay on his feet even when getting bumped by an offensive line. If it turns out that the kid who you thought had the skills to play Leo ends up on the ground more often than not, you might want to consider moving him inside to defensive tackle.

Linebackers

Although the play of your linebackers might be slightly less crucial in a 4-3 than if you were running a 3-4 defense, it's still vital to have players who can actually tackle someone. If you've been able to effectively teach the fundamentals of tackling to your team, then finding kids who can play the linebacker position should be one of the easier tasks for your defense. The toughest thing might be finding kids who can read keys and make tackles, but one way or another you need some playmakers at the position. Even at the Pop Warner level, today's game is about speed, so having at least one linebacker who can move sideline to sideline is crucial.

That brings us to the first of three linebackers in the 4-3 defense: the middle linebacker, or Mike. In the past, middle linebackers have always been thought of as big, physical, bruising players in the mold of Dick Butkus, Mike Singletary, or Brian Urlacher. They are mean, nasty guys who stalk running backs like a lion on the open plain. Today's game is a little different. Although there is certainly room for physical players who can punish running backs with big hits, middle linebackers must be able to cover the field sideline to sideline. Few players better exemplified this than Ray Lewis in his prime. Along with being a very physical player, the Baltimore Ravens linebacker could track down backs sideline to sideline as well as any player in the NFL.

The middle linebacker will likely be the most important player on your defense, and realistically he should be the fastest of all your linebackers at this level. He doesn't necessarily need to be super strong or intimidating, but he should be able to run downhill and make plays. This is the kind of kid who will look good on film, and while part of that is speed, an even bigger part is natural instincts. It is said that great middle linebackers have a "nose for the football," so keep an eye on which kids always seem to be around the ball. Mike linebackers should be good at reading plays, so good vision is a must. Players who are easily fooled by play-action fakes probably will not make the best middle linebackers. That doesn't mean you shouldn't give every kid a chance to play the position at some point; you never know which ones might surprise you with their instincts.

On the outside of a 4-3 defense are strong-side and weak-side line-backers, also known as the Sam and Will linebackers. The Sam backer is responsible for playing the strong side of the field, which means he typically lines up over the offense's tight end. You shouldn't have to worry about too many size matchups at this level, but eventually Sam linebackers will need to have some size, and more importantly height, because they will go up against tall, pass-catching tight ends. Typically, Sam backers can be a little slower than Mikes or Wills, as they will often play closer to the line of scrimmage. Strong-side linebackers have 2-gap responsibility and must be able to handle counters because teams will often run them toward the strong side of the field.

On the other side is the Will linebacker, or weak-side backer, who operates much like the old weak-side defensive end. This can be a kid who might not be as strong, or even as fast, as some of the other kids, but who uses good footwork and takes solid angles. Will linebackers don't have a lot of responsibility up front, but they must be able to help the defensive ends with outside contain while also picking up swing passes and quick slants. This doesn't need to be a kid who's going to make 100 tackles, but you would like to have your Will linebacker make some plays against the run and the pass. Most kids on your team can play this position, so it is an excellent way to get them involved on the defense if you're struggling to find a position for a young player.

Secondary

Establishing your plans to run a 4-3 defense technically takes care of only the front seven. You can use a number of different looks in the secondary, or defensive backfield, but most likely you're going to want a standard look that includes two cornerbacks and two safeties (free and strong). We recommend using a Cover-3 look in the secondary, with three defensive backs responsible for covering the deep portion of the field.

Cornerbacks   Cornerback is one of the most important positions on the field. Your two cornerbacks will primarily be asked to cover the opposing team's top two receivers. Often much smaller than the wide outs they are covering, corners should be athletic and have good timing. Corners are typically associated with having blazing speed à la Deion Sanders, but what corners really need at this level is balance and coordination. Some of your fastest kids will struggle with the concept of running backward and changing direction simultaneously, which all good corners must be able to do in order to play man-to-man coverage. Although you'd love to have corners who can play against the run, stopping the pass is always their number one priority. Teach them never to turn their backs on the quarterback and to read receivers when the ball is in the air.

Safeties   Behind the cornerbacks are the two safeties, and they are the last line of defense. The two different types of safeties, strong safety and free safety, should take the field with the mentality that nothing (i.e., deep passes) gets over their heads. Like an outfielder in baseball, a safety's first step should always be back as he should assume that every play is a deep pass play until his reads tell him differently.

That holds especially true for the free safety, who plays deeper than anyone else on the defense. Great free safeties are typically good ball hawks, so you might be able to identify your best free safety by watching which kid always seems to make a play on the ball when it's in the air. However, be sure that kid is not getting out of position to do so. The last thing in the world you want at the free safety position is a player who takes big gambles in going for the football. His primary job is to provide help for the corners and linebackers over the top while defending the deep part of the field from anything long. He should have good range, have solid speed, and be an excellent open-field tackler.

The strong safety is a bit of a hybrid player who should be able to cover but must also be able to hit. He will be closer to the line of scrimmage and can be used as a blitzer in some defensive looks. Like the free safety, the strong safety's responsibility is to play the pass first and the run second, but if the key looks like a run—that is, the ball is in the hands of a running back moving toward the line of scrimmage—the strong safety becomes a downhill player. In that case, the strong safety must fill the alley, at which point he takes on the responsibilities of a fourth linebacker. There are also times where you will bring him down into the box to help against a dominant running team, so like your linebackers, this kid cannot be afraid of contact. Some of the biggest hits come from the strong safety position, but it's more important that he be a sure tackler than a big hitter because of what it means if he misses.

Game Plan

We recommend running a Cover-3 defense on the back end, which is designed to prevent giving up the big play defensively. Youth football teams are much less likely to sustain a long, double-digit play drive than they are to get lucky on a long play that gets behind the defense because of poor coverage or missed tackles, but it also works well because it is the simplest concept out of which to make adjustments.

The Cover 3 is a zone look with man principles, meaning your defenders should go into man coverage against anyone who enters their zone. Three players are responsible for covering the deep part of the field, and depending on how the opposing offense lines up, your defense could look like a Cover 2 before the snap if they're lined up against a balanced look offensively (see figure 6.4). Your defensive backs must be able to recognize which is the strong side of the field and which is the weak side. The side with more players, typically including a tight end, is the strong side. This tells the defensive backs what their responsibilities are. If the quarterback rolls to the right (see figure 6.5), the front-side safety would have the deep outside third, the back-side safety would have deep middle, and the back-side corner would have the deep portion of the field on the far side (opposite the direction of the quarterback's roll). (Figure 6.6 provides the coverage if the quarterback rolls to the left.) Whether the quarterback rolls to the left or right, the back side flat may be left open, but that is a low danger area when the quarterback is rolling away from that side of the field, especially when the opposing coach does not know what defense you're running. For that very reason, you should try to change up your look defensively even if you're not changing the scheme. Although we don't recommend blitzing very often, it's not a bad idea to show blitz (see figure 6.7) and then have that player drop back into coverage. Do everything you can to confuse the opposing quarterback without confusing your own players on defense.

This might seem like a lot to ask of young kids, but don't underestimate their intelligence. Look at what they do in school or how quickly they can

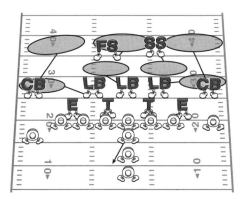

Figure 6.4 Cover-3 defense when the quarterback drops straight back.

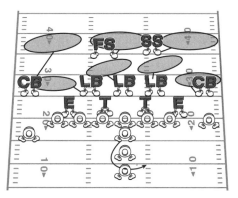

Figure 6.5 Cover-3 defense when the quarterback rolls to the right.

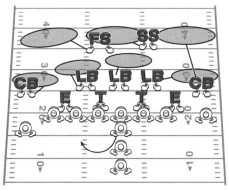

Figure 6.6 Cover-3 defense when the quarterback rolls to the left.

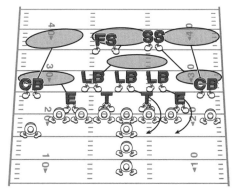

Figure 6.7 Cover-3 defense with a blitz.

master video games. You may even want to use terminology from the *Madden NFL* game. Although most of these kids have not played real football before, many have mastered the art of the virtual game. Prepare your defense for what they're going to see from the opposing offense. Print out a sheet with formations so that your players will recognize them when they see them on the field. Start with the formations your team runs offensively. At this level, most offensive playbooks will be similar, so having your defense prepared to stop what your own offense is running should help prepare the defenders for what they will see from the other teams in your league.

Once the players have an understanding of what these formations look like on paper, make sure they can visualize how they will look on the field. Let the defense know what formation your offense is lined up in during the scrimmage portion of practice. That will help both sides of the ball because your offense will have to work even harder against a defense that already knows how they are lining up. It will be an even bigger help to the defense, however, as they start to understand tendencies and which formations are run heavy or pass heavy. Teach them to read keys, or at least start the process of understanding what it means to read keys. If you're lucky, you might have a few really smart players on your defense who can lead the way for you. If you're even luckier, those players will end up at middle linebacker and one of the two safety spots, which are typically the two leadership positions on a defense. (Eventually, the Mike linebacker will call the plays defensively, and the safeties will set the coverages, but you won't get into that at this level). Instead, teach your linebackers to read the backs and the offensive line. Running backs are usually easiest to read, especially at this level, but it takes a split-second longer than reading the offensive line. If there are no backs in the backfield (rare in youth football), slide your other safety over close to a wide out, and maintain zone principles.

Although some plays can be designed to look deceiving (e.g., traps, counters, reverses), offensive linemen are typically anything but. As a general rule of thumb, if a lineman's first step is forward, it's probably going to be a run play. If his initial step is back, he's probably trying to get between his man and the quarterback, which tells your defense it's likely to be a pass. Certainly, there are exceptions to that rule, and as we said earlier, your safeties should assume pass on every play, regardless, until they see enough to tell them otherwise. The better your players get at recognizing run versus pass, the better your defense will play. Have your defense yell it out in practice—*run, run, run* or *pass, pass, pass*—and have your linebackers alert the secondary once the ball has crossed the line of scrimmage. Again, it all might seem like a bit much, but if you take the time to teach this during practice, most of the kids will pick it up.

If you're fortunate enough to have a large football team to work with, practicing your defense shouldn't be a problem. You might be tempted to have your four best players start both ways, but remember this is not all about winning. If you've got enough kids to run a full offense and a full defense, do it. It will be a huge benefit in getting both sides ready for action. More likely, however, you're going to find yourself with fewer than 22 players. Some teams might have only 11 or 12 kids, in which case you will have to run half-line scrimmages in practice, where you work on one side of the field first and then the other.

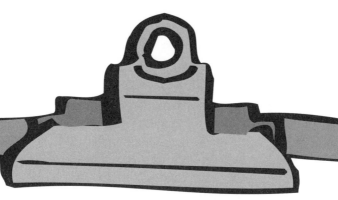

The Coach's Clipboard

✔ The two most traditional defenses are the 4-3 defense (four down linemen and three linebackers) and the 3-4 defense (three down linemen and four linebackers).

✔ Check with the varsity football coach in your community to see what defense they are running at the high school level.

✔ Weak-side linebackers are often called Wills, strong-side linebackers are called Sams, and middle linebackers are Mikes.

✔ The strong side of the field refers to the side with more offensive players, while the weak side refers to the side with fewer offensive players.

✔ Teaching kids to blitz could leave your defense exposed to the big play.

✔ Disrupting the offense is the primary goal of the defensive line.

✔ The Cover 3 is a zone look with man principles, meaning your defenders should go into man coverage against anyone who enters their zone.

Special Teams and Special Plays

In Little Rock, Arkansas, lives a coach named Kevin Kelley. Although Kelley's Pulaski Academy Bruins have enjoyed more than 100 wins this decade, it's not his success that makes him distinctive as much as it his method. Nicknamed a "mad scientist" by those close to the Pulaski football program, Kelley has a unique approach to special teams: He ignores them completely. According to an article in the September 21, 2009, issue of *Sports Illustrated*, Kelley's team has not punted since 2007 (when it did so as a gesture of sportsmanship in a lopsided game), and they have no plans of doing so in the near future.

After meeting with economist David Romer in 2005, Kelley determined that the odds of converting on fourth down outweighed the reward for punting the ball, especially when punts only net about 30 yards at the high school level. Kelley doesn't even bother to keep a punter or kicker on the roster (his teams always go for 2 points after touchdowns). It's a radical coaching philosophy, but there is a lot of truth behind the madness. Although Kelley's nonkicking philosophy, which also includes kicking the ball out of bounds or attempting an onside kick after a score, would not make much sense at the college and pro levels, the kicking game is so wildly inconsistent at the high school level that it almost makes sense. And you can multiply that by 10, or maybe even 100, at the youth level, where kids are still learning the coordination it takes just to get their feet on the ball.

Success with special teams at this level can really become a matter of chance. So many things can go wrong, and at least one usually does. Miss a block on a run play, and your tailback gets knocked down 2 yards in the backfield. Miss a block on a punt, and the other team could be headed for the end zone. We certainly aren't recommending you cut all the kickers and punters from your roster—after all, you shouldn't be making cuts in the first place—but if you decide to kick extra points and field goals, you may find yourself adjusting on the fly when things don't go according to plan.

Kicking

Most leagues don't have kickoffs, but kids need to start understanding the concept of staying in their lanes and not just running to the ball. In most cases, teams will start with the ball at the 30-yard line after a score, and the ball generally goes out to the 45-yard line after a safety. It's still important, however, to practice pursuit drills. This will help your players understand how to track the ball, but it will also help them work on open-field tackling.

You should also have your kids practice extra points, although you will rarely attempt this in a game. At this level, kids are still learning how to use their legs properly, so kicking an extra point can be just as hard as kicking a field goal. In fact your chances are probably better for a 2-point conversion, and as they say, why get 1 when you can go for 2? Field goals are a different story because sometimes you're going to have a heck of a time putting the ball in the end zone for 6 points. Passing the ball in the red zone is always a gamble, and sometimes your offensive line just won't be able to open holes for your running backs. If you happen to be fortunate enough to have a natural-born kicker on your team, then you've already got a leg up on the competition, literally. If not, maybe you can find a soccer player in the neighborhood who wants to try his foot at kicking. A lot of high school teams will even look to the soccer players.

Even if you hit a home run, or more accurately score a goal, by landing a soccer player with some ball skills, you're probably not going to attempt many field goals in crunch time. Too many things can go wrong before the kicker even gets his foot on the ball. First you have to find a kid who can snap the ball. This is a real way for kids who might not have as much skill to make an impact, but you still have to find a kid who can get the ball to the holder on a consistent basis. Nothing is more frustrating as a coach than to watch a snap sail over the holder's head for a turnover at a crucial moment in the game.

There are two ways to avoid snapping mishaps or at least limit them to practice-only miscues. The first is to let every kid on the team try his hand at long snapping and then pick the best one regardless of whether that kid also happens to be your star wide receiver or primary tailback. The other way to find a long snapper is to keep an eye out for kids who might have a knack for it but don't really fit many other places on the football field. These are the kids who will immerse themselves in becoming a better long snapper if it means they can contribute to the team. Unlike your star wide out, who needs to spend most of his time working with the quarterbacks, this player will be able to commit time every day in practice solely to working on perfecting his snap. Obviously, if you don't see the kind of progress you are hoping for, then you will need to find a few more players who can give it a try, but hopefully the harder your long snapper works, the better he will get and the more trust you will have in him.

Oftentimes backup quarterbacks will make good long snappers, but they also make good holders, especially if you want to add a trick play to your arsenal here or there. So do receivers, for the obvious reason that they are good at catching the ball. The key to being a good holder is having a feel for the football. Holders must catch the snap and get it down quickly while making sure the laces of the football are pointing out and not in toward the kicker.

If all of that goes right, you still have to get good blocking up front just to have a chance at making a field goal—and the ball is about as likely to go straight up in the air as it is to go through the uprights. This isn't to say that your kicking game can't progress as the season goes along, but expecting kids to hit game-winning 35-yard field goals at the end of regulation is a bit delusional. Start small. Don't ask a lot of your young kickers or rely on them for much help early on, but don't completely ignore them either. Remember, this isn't about you. This really isn't even about your team. It's about the kids, and doing what's best for them and their future should always be your primary focus.

On the rare occasion when you are brave enough to trot your kicker out there for a field goal, or even an extra point, it's important to get lined up right or you will find out very quickly how easy it is to have a kick blocked. For kicks, your team will want to line up in a tight formation with the long snapper in the center and very small splits between offensive linemen (see figure 7.1). All but two of your players (kicker and holder) will line up on or very close to the line of scrimmage with the holder lined up seven yards behind the center.

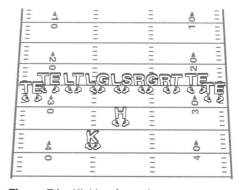

Figure 7.1   Kicking formation.

Punting

Although you can get away with not having a solid kicking game at this level, it doesn't work the same way with punting, unless of course you happen to be Kevin Kelley. Ohio State head coach Jim Tressel has a much different idea about punting. He won five NCAA National Championships—four at Youngstown State and one in Columbus—behind the philosophy that the punt is the most important play in football.

It's not an exciting play, unless something goes wrong, but winning the battle for field position is crucial when points are at a premium. Teams that are forced to "go for it" on fourth-down conversions because they don't trust their punter are at a serious disadvantage; if they don't get the first down, they give the opposing team excellent field position. Kelley's teams may convert half their fourth-down conversions, but the chances of your offense being ready to do that are slim. Having a punter who can push the other team back inside their own territory is a tremendous advantage for your defense, and it will mean fewer headaches for you because you won't have to watch the opposing offense drive 30 yards or less for a touchdown. Finding a player who can net you 20 or 30 yards consistently on a punt won't be easy with kids this age, but if you spend enough time looking, you might actually be surprised what will turn up.

Punting Formation

Finding a player who can punt the ball is only half the battle. You also have to find someone who can snap it, but just as important, you've got to make sure you can block it. You're better off following in Kelley's footsteps when it comes to punting if you aren't able to keep the opposing team's rush from getting to your punter.

Setting up for your punt, you will need seven players on the line every time. That's true about every play in football, but it's a lot easier to forget when you're lining up in a punt formation. A good punt formation, such as the one shown in figure 7.2, should have a long snapper in the middle, two guards to the outside of him, two tackles beyond that, and two ends on the outside (basically the same as a double tight end formation). You might be familiar with formations that have gun-

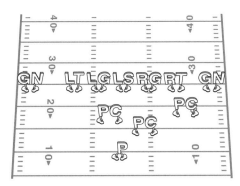

Figure 7.2 Punting formation.

ners lined up out wide like receivers, but there is no need for a spread punt in youth football. Your primary goal on every punt should be to protect the punter at all costs. You don't want to get your splits (the area between each set of linemen) too wide or players will come right up the middle; but also avoid making them too narrow or someone will come from the outside and get the block. Your linemen should step with the outside foot, as they are responsible for their outside gap.

Behind the seven linemen are three punt coverage players who are sometimes affectionately termed "the three monkeys." Two of them should be to the side of the punter's kicking foot (right side for a right-footed punter, left side for a left-footed punter), with the third monkey on the other side. The primary responsibility of all three monkeys is to pick up anyone who gets free inside. If a punt gets blocked up the middle, your monkeys aren't doing their jobs. These three punt coverage players act as a barricade, a wall protecting the punter from all harm that might come his way. They don't have to be the best blockers on your team, but they should be smart football players who can play with the kind of low base necessary to absorb an oncoming rusher. The last thing you want to see is one of your three monkeys getting pushed back into the punter.

Punt Coverage

Protecting the punter and allowing him to get off a clean punt is the most important thing for your blockers, but once the ball is up and away, it's important that they quickly transition to punt coverage (see figure 7.3). It doesn't do a whole lot of good for your team if they block well enough to get the punt off, only to allow the other team's return man to bring it right back into your territory. At this level, the one guy who should be off and running after the snap is the long snapper. In most youth football leagues, the center cannot be hit, which means he will get a free release down the field. This is a huge advantage over the way things are done at the higher levels. It's vital to find a long snapper who can get the ball to the punter consistently, but if you come across a kid who can do that and also run well (and maybe even tackle), you have a true diamond in the rough.

Ideally, your long snapper should be a good athlete, which

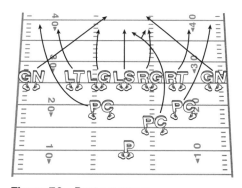

Figure 7.3   Punt coverage.

will allow him to be the first one down the field on coverage. The two ends on the line have outside contain, so they need to get wide and prevent the return man from going down the sideline. The two tackles just inside the contain players have the next inside lanes and so on. We talked earlier about players staying in their lanes, and it's just as important on punt coverage as it is on kickoff. This is something you will need to work on with your players. Even if you tell them exactly where to go, inevitably kid nature will take over, and they will all run directly toward the football. Teach them what it means to stay in a lane all the way down the field, and have them run it over and over in practice (or as often as you can afford with the time you're allotted) until it becomes second nature.

Trick Punt

It's probably not a great idea to spend too much of your valuable practice time working on trick plays that are likely to treat your opponent better than they treat you, but it's not a bad idea to have a few on file. You might end up finding it easier to just line up and go for it outright if you believe your team truly needs to pick up a key first on fourth down, but if you can pull off a trick punt at this level, you should completely fool the opposing coach, not to mention his players.

There are a thousand different ways to run a punt fake, but you're going to want to simplify things for your kids as much as possible. We recommend working on one fake run play and one fake pass play so that you have the option of doing one or the other depending on how you anticipate the other team's punt return will look. There's no need to get fancy with the names if you've got only one run play and one pass play.

For the run play, we recommend a direct snap to the middle punt coverage player (or monkey) as shown in figure 7.4. If you want to teach your punter to sell the fake, have him jump up in the air and act as if the snap went over his head or reach down to the ground as if the ball is in the grass. Either way, your middle monkey, who is now your ballcarrier, should run off tackle behind your best blocker. Make sure the ball-carrier knows how many yards he needs to get, and then just tell him to run toward daylight, follow his blocks, and get to the first-down sticks. Unlike most trick plays, there's not a lot that can go wrong here, except of course if he doesn't happen to get the first down.

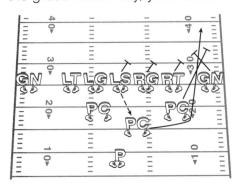

Figure 7.4   Trick punt run play.

The fake pass play involves a bit more risk (see figure 7.5). This is almost always true of a pass versus a rush, but it's even more magnified when it happens on fourth down and it's not your quarterback making the throw. Instead, the snap will actually go to your punter, which helps keep the fake hidden a little longer than with the run play. Your punter should still act as if he's

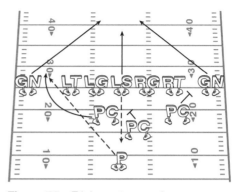

Figure 7.5 Trick punt pass play.

going to punt, but instead, he will throw a pass to the back-side blocker in the opposite flat. That back-side blocker should be able to slip out into the flat as if he's playing contain on the coverage, and unless you've run this same play before in the game, he should be wide open for the pass. Now it's just a matter of getting the ball to him.

Special Plays

The risk-to-reward ratio for trick plays is not very high, but you never know when you might desperately need one to keep a game, or even a season, alive. In 2007, Boise State found itself in that exact situation in the Fiesta Bowl against heavily favored Oklahoma. After trailing for much of the game, the Sooners scored 25 unanswered points in the second half, including 15 in the final 1:26 of regulation, to take a 35-28 lead. Down by 7 with seven seconds to play, Broncos coach Chris Peterson pulled out his book of trick plays and went with an old faithful: the hook and ladder (hook and lateral). Quarterback Jared Zabransky connected with Drisan James on a 15-yard curl route, and James lateraled the ball to Jerard Rabb as he came running by on the end of his route. Rabb went the final 35 yards for a 50-yard touchdown play that tied the game and sent it into overtime.

But the Sooners weren't done yet, and neither were the Broncos. After Oklahoma took the lead on a touchdown in overtime, Boise State tied the game on a wide receiver pass from Vinny Perretta to Derek Schouman on fourth and 2. An extra point would have sent the game into double overtime, but Peterson opted instead for another trick play. It really was a roll of the dice for Boise State, but Peterson dialed up the perfect call, with Zabransky handing off behind his back to running back Ian Johnson, who went untouched into the end zone for the winning score. The play is known as the Statue of Liberty, and it's nothing new to football. Legendary coach Amos Alonzo Stagg is credited for first using the play

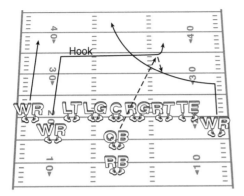

Figure 7.6 Hook and ladder play.

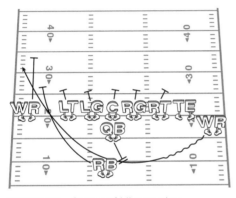

Figure 7.7 Statue of Liberty play.

at the University of Chicago in the early 1900s, but few people had actually seen it run like that with their own two eyes.

These are plays you can theoretically learn with enough practice. The key to a good hook and ladder is that one player runs a hook, or a curl route, 10 to 15 yards down the field, and another player times his route perfectly so that he is running full speed just behind the player who makes the catch (see figure 7.6). Ideally, the play will put the defense out of position by having them react to the first player, and by the time the second player receives the flip, he will be long gone before the defense has a chance to adjust. It worked perfectly for Boise State; it might not go as smoothly for your team the first time you run it.

The same goes for the Statue of Liberty play (see figure 7.7). The key to this play is the quarterback's forcing the defense to think he is going to throw the ball before he gives it to the running back. The quarterback should start under center with two hands on the ball. As he drops back, he should plant and fake with his throwing arm while holding the ball behind his back with his nonthrowing hand. The key to the play is the defense's falling for the pump fake, while a running back or wide receiver snags the football from the quarterback's off hand and takes off in the opposite direction. If the defense isn't fooled, or if the guy taking the ball from the quarterback isn't paying attention to detail, you could end up with a sack or a fumble, but that's the nature of trick plays. Most of them are high risk, high reward.

If you're going to run one of these plays in a game, you're going to have to practice them every time you have practice. It might seem like a lot of concentration for a play you might run once in a game, but these kinds of plays are fun for the kids. Even if you never end up running them, it's a great exercise for building morale. Run it at the end of every practice, and it will give the kids something to look forward to. They will be excited to practice it, and if you ever run it in a game, you're going to have to call it early in the play clock so you have enough time to curb their enthusiasm and grab their focus.

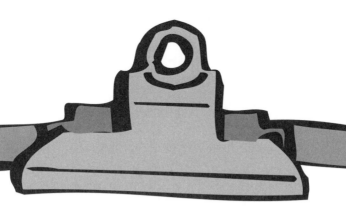

The Coach's Clipboard

✔ Most leagues don't have kickoffs, but kids need to start understanding the concept of staying in their lanes and not just running to the ball.

✔ Skilled soccer players could make good kickers on the football field.

✔ Find kids who excel at long snapping, and have them make it their passion.

✔ The punt can often be the most important play in a game.

✔ There must be seven players on the line of scrimmage for every play, even punts and kicks.

✔ Protecting the punter and allowing him to get off a clean punt is more important than getting downfield on coverage.

✔ Ideally, your long snapper should be a good athlete, which will allow him to be the first one down the field on coverage.

✔ Even if you never use them in a game, practicing trick plays is a good way to make things fun for your players.

Game Time! What's My Role Again?

For many first-time coaches, football is all about control: wanting to control the outcome of the game, wanting to control the players, and wanting to control where the ball goes on every play. This works great for running a practice because a good coach will organize things down to the minute. If the players aren't running a play the right way, or if the ball is not getting to the right person, just call them back to the line and have them run it again until they get it right. An organized coach can generally script a practice that allows him to control every detail down to the excruciating minutia.

The same does not hold true for game days, however. No matter how hard a coach tries to be in control of everything during a game, things are bound to go haywire, and a coach must learn to ride the waves while staying calm, cool, and collected. There are times to micromanage your team, but game days are typically reserved for a more hands-off approach. Obviously, you will have a better idea of just how much coaching your team needs when you get to the first game day, but this is not the time to tighten the reins. One of the hardest things for new coaches to understand is that their role, more often than not, actually shrinks on game day. After days, or in some cases weeks, of training and game planning in practice, it only seems natural for a coach to want to have his hand in everything that happens in the actual games.

Certainly, at the highest levels of football, plenty of adjustments can and should be made by a coach during the course of a game. That's why those coaches are paid the big bucks. Trying to make adjustments on the fly with kids is like trying to reinvent the wheel in a day. It might sound good in theory, but in practice it won't produce many results. As a youth football coach, it's your job to prepare your kids in practice for what they will face in a game, but once the ball is kicked off, it's primarily up to the players to determine the outcome. Coaches like to think they are pulling strings, but no coach has ever thrown a key block, made a tackle, caught a touchdown, or picked up a crucial first down from the sideline.

Defining Your Role

In football more than any other sport, the coach is responsible for calling each play. At the higher levels, quarterbacks are given some leeway with calling their own plays, but you won't be dealing with any of that at this level. The play-calling duties may be up to you, but the execution is still up to your players. You can call the perfect play at the ideal time against a completely unsuspecting defense, but if your quarterback trips over the center's foot or your receiver runs the wrong route, the play could easily turn out to be a disaster. Assuming you prepared your players as best you could in practice, you must realize that you could have done nothing to make the play a success. No matter how frustrating it might seem, you must let these mishaps roll off your shoulders. Chalk it up to your players being 9 years old, and then start planning when you're going to try that perfect play again, hopefully with better results. Resilience is a big part of being a good youth football coach. Those who don't have it or can't learn it usually don't last very long.

One thing you cannot do as a youth football coach, under any circumstances, is embarrass one of your players publicly for making a mistake. Remember, these kids are out there trying their best, and the last thing their fragile psyches need is their coach yelling at them from the sideline in front of friends and family, not to mention their teammates, for making a mistake as a 9-year-old. It's important to keep the ultimate goal in mind. If your primary reason for being out there is to win the game, you're in the wrong place. Coaching kids is often about putting aside your competitive nature—you know, that little voice inside you that says to run out there, grab the ball, and stiff-arm a handful of 9-year-olds into the ground on your way to the end zone—in order to do what's best for them.

That doesn't mean you can't take pride in victory, but there are going to be times—maybe many of them—when you will want to shout and stomp your foot as if you are 9 years old too, but these are nothing more than opportunities to display the self-control that comes with being an adult. If you need to vent about a bad call or a bad play, save it for your spouse, coworkers, or assistant coaches, but don't direct it at the kids or the officials. There may be times where you need to encourage one of your players when he's feeling down or correct him after a key mistake, but it's important to keep these conversations constructive and private. The last thing a young player needs is his coach pulling him off the field by his facemask so he can be yelled at on the sideline.

Managing Pregame Details

Game days can be a hectic time. Who is bringing the orange slices? Are orange slices a cool enough snack for football? Is there enough water available, or will you have to go looking for a hose? Did you remember the footballs? Are any kids missing equipment? Did all the kids use the restroom before putting on their cups? There is so much going on that sometimes the little things that are essentials for every team are overlooked. Figure 8.1 provides a quick checklist of things every coach should do before his players take the field against another squad.

Make up a starting lineup the night before a game, and be sure to make a few copies of your roster (with numbers) if you're going to have a parent out there taking photos or keeping statistics. It's a good idea to have an alternate lineup in place as well. This will help you demonstrate your plan to rotate kids through multiple positions, and it will cover you in case one of your starters is too sick to play that day.

You also need a plan in place for how you're going to get each and every kid into the game. If you have a roster of only 12 to 15 kids, this shouldn't be a problem. If you're fortunate enough to have 20 kids on your team, this might get a little more complicated. The last thing you want to do is leave a kid standing on the sideline for most of the game because you forgot to put him out there. Have a plan. You may need to write it down, but one way or another have an idea for when and where you want to get each kid in the game. You can adjust depending on how the game unfolds, but there is never an excuse for forgetting to play a kid.

Once you arrive at the field, act as if you're running for office. No, don't go around taking up a collection for your campaign, but put yourself out there. Be sure to greet the opposing coaches as well as the referees, and don't forget to socialize with the parents of your own players. Shake hands, kiss a few babies if need be, but it's important to keep things social. This should help to give you solid footing should a dispute arise during the game.

Figure 8.2   Pregame Warm-Up

Get the pregame warm-up under way with a series of light drills covering all the skills and some stretches.

Time to kickoff	Activities
60 minutes to kickoff	Stretching: Use the warm-up routine on page 24.
40 minutes to kickoff	Individual workouts: Break team into different position groups. Have quarterbacks work on their snaps with the centers before warming up their arms by passing with a partner. Have receivers practice running routes while someone throws passes to them. Have running backs practice taking hand-offs. Offensive linemen should work on their footwork.
25 minutes to kickoff	Water break: Everyone on the team should get water so that the players aren't asking for it individually.
20 minutes to kickoff	Offensive and defensive strategy: Break the team into offense and defense, and run through plays that will be used in the game. Talk about what the opposing team is going to do, and make sure all 11 players are on the same page.
5 minutes to kickoff	Water break: Everyone on the team should get water. Some kids will say they don't need it, but everyone needs it.
Game time	Have fun, and encourage your players to have fun!

the players, and reassure them of what is going to happen, especially if this is the first game of the season. Cover each of the following topics:

- **The starting lineup.** If you're following our advice, this is something that should change each game, so be sure to let the players know who will be starting (assuming you have more than 11 players on your team). Even if you plan to play all your players—and you most certainly should—the temptation will be there to start your best players every game, but youth football is about getting experience, so try to get every kid into the starting lineup during your season. If you have more than 11 players, make sure your starters know they aren't going to play the entire game. Simulate substitutions during practice so you don't end up with too many men on the field or kids who refuse to come off the field. You might be tempted to use a bad play as an excuse for getting one of your subs in the game, but we would caution you against that method. Although these are excellent teachable moments, yanking a kid off the field after he makes a mistake is not the best way to teach. Wait for the appropriate time to make substitutions.

- **The game plan.** You spent all of practice telling your players how you want to attack the other team, but that doesn't mean they will remember that this is the time and the place. (Sometimes putting two and two together ends up equaling five in their minds.) This is a good time to review a few quick things such as the snap count on offense and assignments on defense.

- **The fun factor.** Remind your players that football is a game and is meant to be fun. Some will be nervous about having to perform, so reassure them that having fun and trying hard are the two most important things. Alert them to the fact that not everything is going to go perfectly and that no one should get down on themselves over making a mistake. Football games are not won and lost on one play, but rather the outcomes are determined by the sum of all plays during the game.

- **Questions.** There might be a feeling that as soon as you have spoken your piece, the kids will feel at ease and things are ready to begin. In reality, their little heads are probably still full of questions, and it's a good idea to ask for them at this time. Inevitably, at least one kid will ask if he can get the ball on the first play, to which your response should always be *We'll see*.

Once the game officially starts, your role is as much a cheerleader as it is a coach. The players will certainly need direction, but they will also need encouragement. It is one thing to make a mistake in practice, but making a mistake in front of friends and parents during a game will be extra hard on some of your players. By now, you should have an idea of which kids might come to tears over dropping a touchdown catch, though you may be surprised by which ones have a hard time dealing with failure in a game situation. They will be looking to you now more than ever. It's important to remind the kids that trying hard and having fun are the most important things. Be sure to applaud them for giving extra effort, and don't be afraid to pull a kid aside and put your arm around him if he is having a tough time with his mistakes. Just be sure not to coddle those kids too much.

A big part of sports is teaching life lessons, and some of these kids have never been forced to deal with failure on their own before. As their coach, your job is to tread the thin line between encouraging and babying. If you have a kid who really gets upset over making a mistake or losing a game, you might be tempted to make sure he is always on the winning team during practice. Unfortunately, your good intentions might actually be doing him a disservice. Most of the players on your team, however, will do just fine being showered with praise. Just view every mistake as an opportunity to teach, and you will be just fine. After all, isn't that what coaching really is? If a kid drops a pass because he is using the wrong technique, instead of yelling at him as he comes off the field, take a moment to remind him of what he learned in practice, and reassure him that he will have a better chance at making the catch next time if he remembers to use the right method. Keep in mind that these kids are young, and they are just learning how to play the game the right way.

Putting Winning in Perspective

Let's be honest, winning is fun. It's fun for you, for the kids, and for the parents. No one likes to lose, especially not the parents. Even if you explain to them in the preseason parents meeting that youth football is not about winning, there will still be parents who think you should win every game. They want what's best for their kid and tend to get a little delusional about how good he might actually be. It's OK for parents to be gung ho about winning, just as long as it doesn't put pressure on the kids to be perfect or on you, the coach, to start doing things that do not fit with the goals of the team.

Don't lose sight of why you are here. Youth football is not about winning at all costs. If that were your goal, you would have chosen a different venue for coaching. This is supposed to be about trying hard, having fun, and learning the game. If you lose sight of that, everyone loses, even the parents who think winning is what's most important. Keep winning in perspective. After all the time spent in practice, your players are going to want to win, but no team wins every time out (even the 2007 Patriots couldn't win them all).

Losing isn't fun. In fact, some of your players are going to have a very tough time with it. There may be tears. There may even be anger. It's OK to be disappointed. In fact, some of these players might need a good loss or two under their belts to toughen them up and get them past the idea that winning is easy. No matter how talented your team may be, nothing good comes without hard work. Sometimes the best reminder of what it takes to win can be a loss. As a youth football coach, your job is to teach your young players how to lose with dignity. This will be important for their future development as athletes, but it is also a vital life skill that often gets overlooked in the classroom, especially in today's society where they hand out ribbons for 10th place and kids get as many chances as they need to pass a test. These are not necessarily bad things, but they can create a culture in which kids are not equipped to deal with the realities of failure.

If you want to teach kids how to avoid being sore losers, then you had better walk the walk and not just talk the talk. Kids will almost always do as you do and not as you say. That means taking losses in stride by turning negatives into positives. Don't let it get under your skin if things aren't going your way. Sometimes it's just not your day, but even when things seem to be clicking on all cylinders, there are still going to be tougher, stronger, and faster teams that just have your number. Don't sweat the things that are out of your control. If you throw your hands in the air or toss your clipboard in disgust, you may not realize it, but you are sending a message that it's OK to be a poor sport when things aren't going your way. Some negative reactions to losing aren't as obvious as tossing a clipboard, but they are equally damaging. Scowls and silence speak loudly, so don't stop coaching just because your team is behind. Take advantage of the teaching opportunities presented in these situations, and let your players know how they can make a better decision or better play next time or next game.

As important as it is to learn how to lose with dignity, it is equally imperative to teach your kids to win with class. Obviously, winning feels good, and it can be a great bonding experience for players to celebrate with their teammates, but teach them not to rub victory in the faces of those on the opposite sideline. Remind them of what it feels like to be on the losing end of a tough ball game and how angry it can make them when someone from the winning side is gloating about the victory. The same goes for you, Coach. Sure, you may not be out there jumping around pumping your fist in the air after a big win, but often times the final score is a good indication of whether or not you decided to win with class. Certainly, you want to keep a team down and put them away before you pull the foot off the gas (if you once make the mistake of letting up too early, you'll never do it again), but beating a team 100-0 is simply unacceptable behavior for a youth football coach.

Even if you are convinced that your team is the worst collection of talent to step foot on the gridiron in recent human history, you will undoubtedly run into a team along the way that is even worse, possibly much worse. Considering the inconceivable nature of this event, you may be caught off guard as you watch your group of future chess All-Americans march up and down the field at will. Take this moment to encourage your team, and praise them for their hard work and good play, but don't forget to keep an eye on the scoreboard so that things don't get too out of hand. Close every game by having your team slap high fives and say *good game* to their opponents.

Working With the Officials

One of the strangest relationships in all of sports is that of a coach and a referee. If ever there were a true tale of love and hate, this would be it. When things are going your way, the guys in black and white stripes are a coach's best friend, but inevitably things won't stay that way for too long. Calls that went your team's way in the first half are bound to go against you in the second half or the next game or the game after that. If you coach long enough—and by long enough we mean more than a game or two—your team is bound to find itself on the wrong side of a bad call. If you are putting the best interest of your players first, a bad call here or there should be relatively easy to get over, but what happens when things start to pile up? What happens when a single bad call becomes 5 (perceived) bad calls or even 10? It's one thing to lose to a superior opponent, but one of the toughest things for coaches to deal with at any level is the idea that your team is getting squeezed or in some way shafted by the referees. Although referees are expected to be impartial—and the vast, vast majority of them truly are, especially at this level—it can be exasperating to watch someone who never throws a pass, makes a block, scores a touchdown, or records a tackle have such a drastic impact on the outcome of a game.

Understandably, even the calmest coaches would start to get a little hot under the collar after a while, and some parents won't even wait that long. Even if you followed our advice by having a preseason parents meeting where you outlined acceptable behavior for the season, chances are good that one of them will inevitably lose his cool over a bad call. It's important to let unruly parents know that this type of behavior will not be accepted, but only if you have a leg to stand on. If five minutes earlier you were yelling at a ref for making a bad call, correcting one of the parents for doing the same would be hypocritical.

As a youth football coach, everything you say and do on game days will be under a microscope. That might scare you, but it shouldn't if your heart is in the right place. Remember the golden rule, do unto others . . . well, you know the rest, but it's important to keep these things in mind when dealing with officials. You should also keep in mind that most of the refs are volunteers or at the very least getting paid minimally for what they do. Like you, and your players, they are out there getting experience and trying their best. It's one thing to expect NFL refs to get the call right every time, but the guys in Pee Wee are still learning what it takes to be a good referee, so cut them a little slack the same way you would want people to cut you slack as a first-time coach.

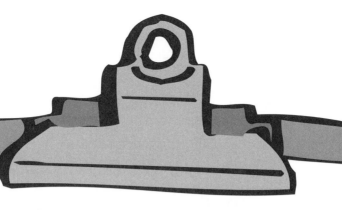

The Coach's Clipboard

✔ Game days are as uncontrollable as they are unpredictable.

✔ It's your job to call the plays, whether that's from the sideline or inside the huddle (depends on your league).

✔ Don't let your competitive nature get the best of you—this is about the kids.

✔ Never embarrass a player for making a mistake during a game.

✔ Make up a starting lineup the night before a game, and be sure to make a few copies of your roster (with numbers).

✔ Have a plan in place for how you're going to get each and every kid into the game.

✔ Remind your players to hit the bathrooms before the game.

✔ Don't preach; speak to the kids on their level.

✔ Remind your players that football is a game and is meant to be fun.

✔ Treat the refs, players, and coaches with the same respect you want to be treated with.

About the Authors

Jim Dougherty knows how to develop talent across many levels. Along with coaching the Hilliard Davidson varsity baseball team since 1985, Dougherty has served as the athletic coordinator and football coach for Hilliard Weaver Middle School since 1997. Prior to that, Dougherty held the same position at the former Hilliard Middle School. He also teaches physical education and was named Ohio's Middle School Athletic Administrator of the Year in 2005. A graduate of Ohio Wesleyan University, he served as the captain of both the football and baseball team. Coach Dougherty lives in Columbus.

Brandon Castel is a sports writer for the-Ozone.net and has made a career of covering college football. While a student at Ohio State, Castel served as the sports editor of *The Lantern* and today he covers the Buckeyes on a full-time basis for BuckeyeGrove.com. A former football player himself, Castel also fills much of his time as a coach in Columbus with the Skyhawks youth sports program. His writing has been featured by Yahoo! Sports, *The Sporting News*, and USCHO.com.